Rhythms

OrangeBooks Publication

Smriti Nagar, Bhilai, Chhattisgarh - 490020

Website: **www.orangebooks.in**

© Copyright, 2024, Author

All rights reserved. No part of this book may be reproduced, stored in a retrieval system, or transmitted, in any form by any means, electronic, mechanical, magnetic, optical, chemical, manual, photocopying, recording or otherwise, without the prior written consent of its writer.

First Edition, 2024

ISBN: 978-93-6554-668-2

RHYTHMS
A PRACTICAL GUIDE TO AN ECG

RASHMI KALSHETTY SONONE

OrangeBooks Publication
www.orangebooks.in

Preface

CONSISTENCY WINS,

Because its not what you do once in a while that matters, Its what you do every day.

This book provides all the information that a medicos like MBBS, allied, BAMS, BHMS, nursing students needs to read an ECGS interpretation.

It covers everything related to the fundamentals of ECG interpretation. The book is simple to understand and a must for everyone in the medical profession engaged in day to day clinical practice. This book is unique because it have a pacemaker and PAEDIATRIC ECGS.

Any errors of omission or commission may kindly be brought to the notice. It will help in improving the subsequent edition.

Very special thanks to my parents suman and Shivaraj Kalshetty. My younger brother Ritesh.

Special thanks to my husband Dr Bhsuhan Sonone (radiologist) in believing in me and helping me to become the best version of myself and always being the best husband and my darling daughter Reesha.

Thank you and grateful to all my guide and guru's Dr Prasad sir (sr. Interventional cardiologist, KLE university).

Bharat Patel sir cardiac sonographer (united states)

Dr Shashank Kulkarni (Pysician and Director of Millenium Institue Dr Vrashli Kulkarni (Paediatrician)

Dr Roopesh Eklarkar (Ex-Senate Member Rguhs/ Principal of Ssamc Dr Mamata H S (Associate Professor Ssamc)

Dr Shakuntala Mam and Veda. For always being there to solve my question and doubts

Author

Rashmi Kalshetty Sonone
Echocardiographer/ Vice
Principal of Allied Institute
TMPS).

Content

1) What Is ECG ? 1
2) ECG Leads 4
3) ECG Rate Interpretation 8
4) Calculating Rate 10
5) Normal ECG 13
6) "P"- Waves 17
7) Pr-Interval 21
8) Pr –Segment 22
9) Q Wave 23
10) Qt – Interval 24
11) 'T'-Wave:- 27
12) Bundle Branch Block 31
13) Left Bundle Branch Block 33
14) Right Bundle Branch Block 37
15) Fascicular Blocks 41
16) Left Posterior Fascicular Block [LPFB] 46
17) Interventricular Conduction Delay (QRS-Widening) 49
18) Bi-Fascicular Block 51

19) Tri-Fascicular Block :- 53
20) First Degree Heart Block 56
21) 2nd Degree, Mobitz I [Wenckbach Phenomenon] 57
22) Complete Heart Block 60
23) Atrial Enlargement 61
24) Cardiac Hypertrophy 66
25) Right Ventricular Hypertrophy 71
26) Cardiomyopathy 73
27) Dilated Cardiomyopathy (DCM) 74
28) Hypertrophy Cardiomyopathy[HCM] 77
29) Restrictive Cardiomyopathy 79
30) ECG In (VSD) Ventricular Septal Defect 82
31) ECG In Atrial Septal Defect (ASD) 85
32) ECG In (PDA) "Patent Ductus Arteriosus". 88
33) ECG In Tof 90
34) ECG In Rheumatic's 92
35) ECG In Mitral Stenosis 98
36) ECG In Aortic Regurgitation 100
37) ECG In Aortic Stenosis :- 103
38) ECG In Tricuspid Stenosis: 106
39) ECG In Tricuspid Regurgitation: 108
40) ECG In Pulmonary Stenosis 110
41) ECG In Pulmonary Regurgitation 112

- **42)** ECG In Dextrocardia 114
- **43)** Ebstein Anomaly 116
- **44)** Coarctation Of The Aorta 118
- **45)** Infective Endocarditis 120
- **46)** Truncus Arteriosus 122
- **47)** ECG Features In Atrial Fibrillations 126
- **48)** Atrial Flutter 128
- **49)** Pre-Mature Atrial Complex 131
- **50)** Benign Early Reproduction 133
- **51)** Beta Blocks Toxicity 135
- **52)** Bi-Directional Ventricular Tachycardia (BVT) 136
- **53)** Brugada Syndrome 138
- **54)** Calcium Channel Blocks Toxicity 140
- **55)** Carbamazepine Cardiotoxicity 141
- **56)** ECG In Copd Chronic Obstructive Pulmonary Disease 142
- **57)** Digoxin Effect 145
- **58)** Digoxin Toxicity 147
- **59)** Hypercalcaemia 148
- **60)** Hyperkalaemia 150
- **61)** Hyperthyroidism 153
- **62)** Hypercalcaemia 155
- **63)** Hypokalaemia 157
- **64)** Hypomagnesaemia 159

65) Hypothermia 161

66) Hypothyroidism 163

67) Intracranial Pressure 165

68) Intrinsicoid Deflection 167

69) Junctional Premature Beat Or Premature Junctional Complex 169

70) LMCA Occlusion : ST Elevation In AVR 171

71) Low QRS Voltage 175

72) ECG Motion Artefacts 177

73) Multifocal Atrial Tachycardia (MAT) 179

74) Myocarditis 181

75) Pacemaker Rhythms –Normal Patterns 183

76) Accelerated Junctional Rhythm 190

77) ECG Limb Lead Reversal 192

78) Sgarbossa Criteria Or Left Bundle Branch Block – Diagnosing Myocardial Infarction. 208

79) Pacemaker Malfunction 212

80) Atrial Tachycardia 215

81) Left Ventricular Aneurysm 217

82) Paediatric ECG Interpretation 220

83) Anterior Myocardial Infarction 241

84) Lateral Stemi 246

85) Inferior Stemi 248

86) Posterior Myocardial Infarction 251

87) Right Ventricular Infarction 254

88) Takotsubo Cardiomyopathy 257

89) LMCA Occlusion : ST Elevation In AVR 260

90) Misplacement Of V1 And V2 263

91) Idiopathic Fascicular Left Ventricular Tachycardia 267

92) Ventricular Tachycardia – Monomorphic (VT) 270

93) Right Ventricular Outflow Tract (RVOT) Tachycardia 275

94) VT Versus SVT 278

What Is ECG?

An electro-cardiogram is a simple, painless test that measures your heart's electrical active.

What happens during ECG procedure?
- It is a quick, painless, harmless procedure.
- Once's a technician attaches 12 to 15 soft electrodes with a gel to your chest, legs, arms.
- Electrodes are attached to the electrical leads (wire) which are then attached to the ECG machine.

During the test, you'll need to lie still on a bed while the machine records your heart's electrical activity and places the information on graph. Make sure to lie as still as possible and breathe normally. You shouldn't talk during the test.

- After the procedure, the electrodes are removed. The entire procedure takes about 10 min.

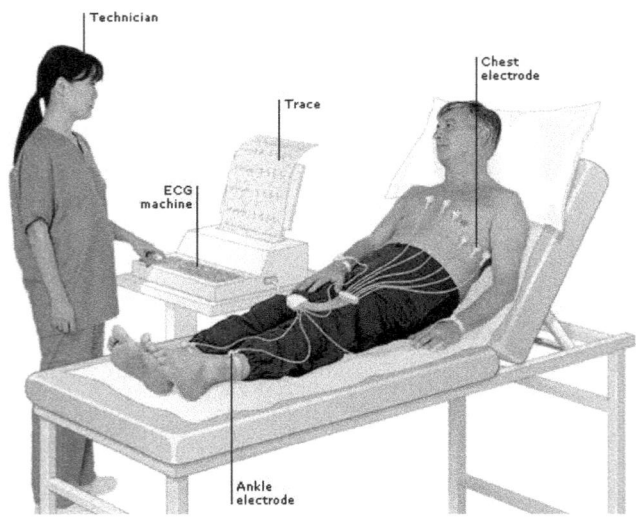

Types of ECG:

An ECG records a picture of your heart's electrical activity for the time that you're being monitored. However, some heart problem's come and go. In these cases, you may need longer or more specialized monitoring.

1) Stress Test.
2) Holter monitor.

1. Stress test:

Some hearts problems only appear during exercise. During stress testing, you'll have an ECG. While you're exercising. typically, this test is done while you're on a treadmill or stationary bicycle.

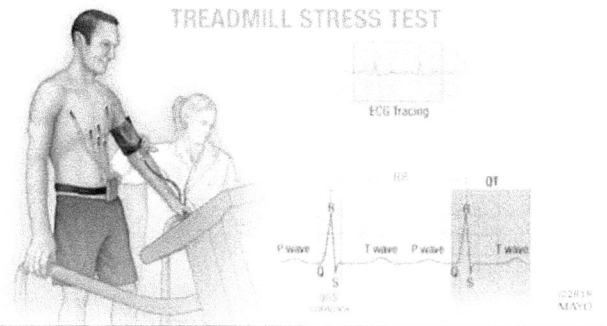

2. Holter monitor:

This is also known as "Ambulance ECG" a Holter monitor records your heart's activity over 24 to 48 hours. While you maintain a dairy of your activity to help your doctor to identify the cause of your symptoms.

Electrodes are attached to your chest record information on a portable battery opertated monitor that you can carry in your pocket, or on a shoulder strap.

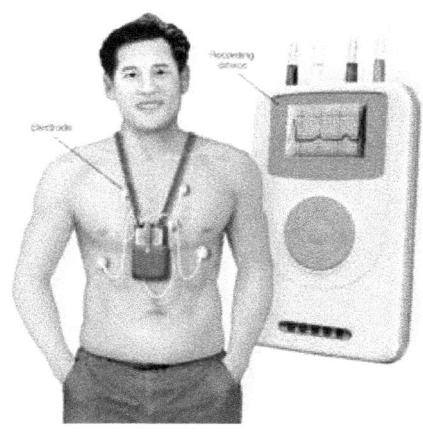

ECG Leads

What are ECG leads?

- An electro-cardiogram uses electrodes attaches to the skin, which are able to detect electrical currents. In order to provide us with information about your heart. The information detected by the electrodes is used to calculate the measurements knows as leads.

- A "lead" is an angle of looking at the heart. A standard ECG includes 12 leads, that 12 different angles of orientation in regards to the heart.

- Each lead provides us with information about different parts of heart.

- A standard ECG typically requires 10 electrodes in order to provide 12 – leads view.

❖ Six limbs on vertical /frontal plane : 3 standard (I, II, III) and 3 augmented (avR, avL, avF)

- V1 , V2 :- Intra ventricular septum

- V3 , V4 :- Anterior wall

- V5 , V6 :- left lateral wall

Rhythms

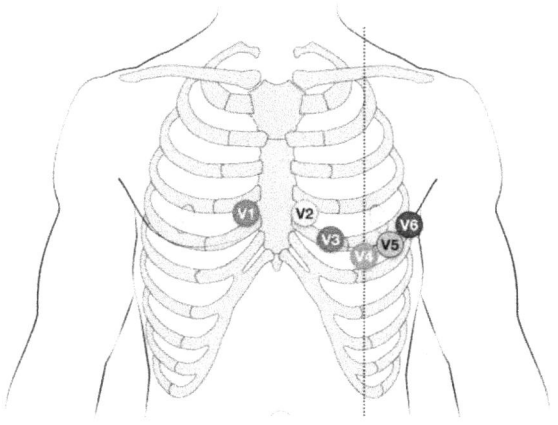

❖ Supplementary leads V7 , V8 , V9.

- Left lateral leads V7, V8, V9 the posterior wall in the area of left ventricle.
- Right pre-cordial leads VR1_9 .

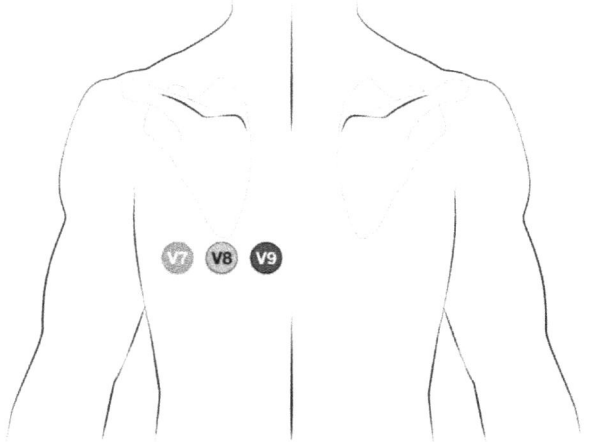

Electrical Axis

Assessment of the Electrical Axis is an integral part of ECG Interpretation. The Electrical Axis reflects the average direction of ventricular depolarization is generally alongside the hearts longitudinal axis.

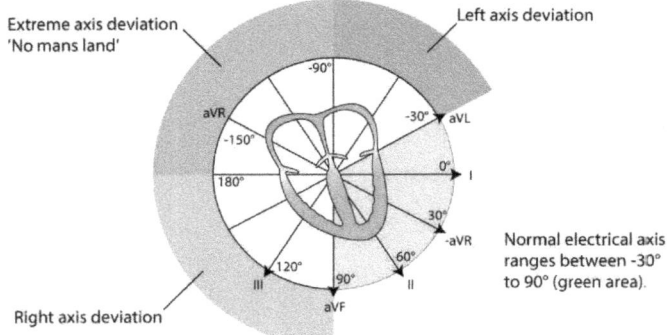

1) The normal heart axis is between is -300 and 900

2) If the axis is more positive them 90 degree it is referred to as right axis deviation.

3) If the axis more negative than - 30 degree it is referred as left axis deviation.

4) If the axis calculated by ECG machine, manually it can be the net QRS complex in lead I and lead II

The Following Rules Apply:

1) Normal axis: net positive QRS complex in lead I and Lead II

2) Right axis deviation: net negative QRS complex in lead I but positive in lead II

3) Left axis deviation: net positive QRS complex in lead I but negative in lead II
4) Extreme axis deviation: 90 degree to 180 degree): net negative QRS complex in lead I and II

ECG Rate Interpretation

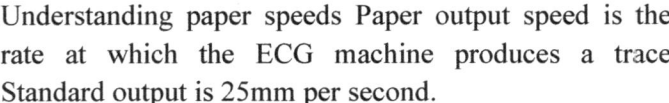

Understanding paper speeds Paper output speed is the rate at which the ECG machine produces a trace Standard output is 25mm per second.

If a different paper speed is used, standard rate calculations will have to be modified appropriately (see other examples below)

The standard paper speed is 25mm/sec:

1 SMALL square (1mm) = 0.04 sec (40ms)

5 SMALL squares (5mm) = 1 LARGE square = 0.2 sec (200ms)

5 LARGE squares = 1 second

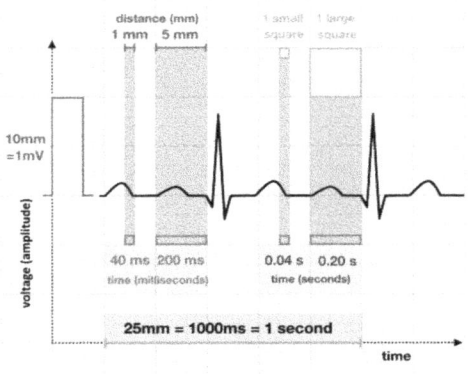

At standard paper speed of 25mm/sec, the rhythm strip comprises of: 250 SMALL squares = 50 LARGE squares = 10 seconds

Before calculating rate in beats per minute (bpm), we should understand that a rhythm strip recorded for 1 minute will therefore compromise:

1500 SMALL squares = 300 LARGE squares = 1 minute

Calculating Rate

There are three main methods of calculating ECG rate. There is no specific best method, and preference varies between clinicians. However, certain methods may be better suited for rhythms such bradyarrhythmias or tachyarrhythmias.

1) Large square method

Recall above that 300 large squares is equal to 1 minute at a paper speed of 25mm/sec

We can thus calculate bpm by dividing 300 by the number of LARGE squares between each R-R interval (space between two consecutive R waves = one beat)

For example, two large squares between each R-R interval implies a rate of 150 bpm, three implies a rate of 100 bpm and so forth:

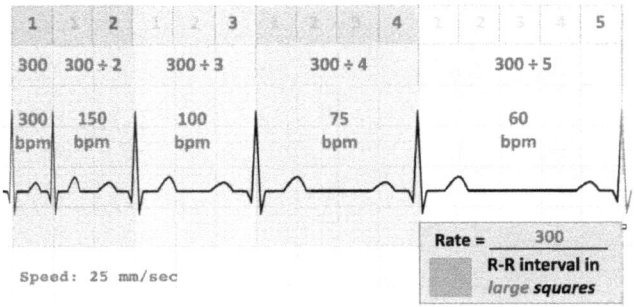

Large square method: Divide 300 by the number of large squares between R-R interval. Useful for regular rhythms Useful as quick calculation for regular rhythms at regular rate

2) Small square method

Similar to above, except 1500 is divided by the number of SMALL squares between consecutive R waves For example, 10 small squares between R-R interval implies a rate of 150 bpm, 15 implies a rate of 100 bpm, and so forth:

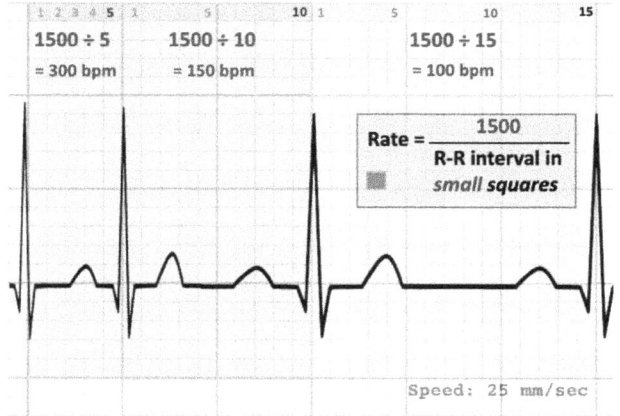

Small square method: Divide 1500 by number of small squares between R-R interval.

Useful for very fast regular rhythms, as likely to provide more accurate rate than large square method.

3) R wave method
Rate = **Number of R waves (rhythm strip) X 6**

The number of complexes (count R waves) on the rhythm strip gives the average rate over a ten-second period. This is multiplied by 6 (10 seconds x 6 = 1 minute) to give the average beats per minute (bpm) Useful for slow and/or irregular rhythms

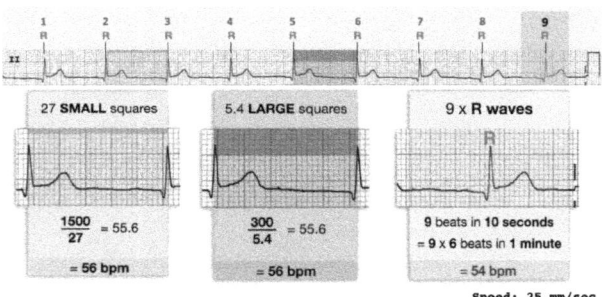

Comparison of three methods: The R wave method is often easiest as a quick calculation.

Normal ECG

Normal ECG :-

A normal ECG contains waves, interval, segments and one complex, as defined below.

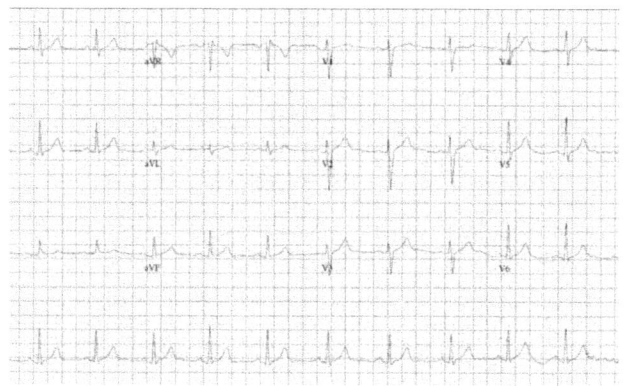

Wave:- A positive wave or negative wave deflection from baseline that indicates one specific electrical event. The waves on an ECG include the P wave, Q wave, 'R' wave, S wave, T wave and U wave.

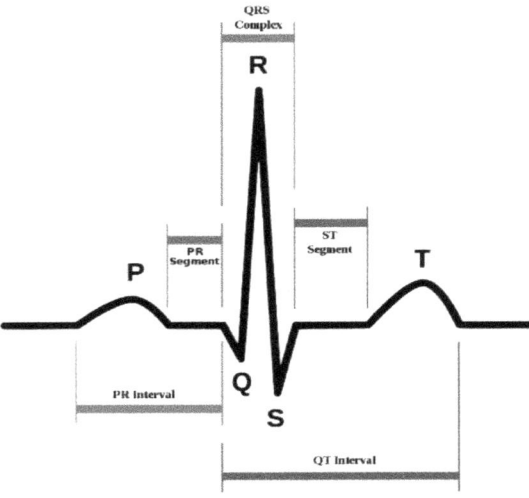

Interval:- The time between two specific ECG events. The interval commonly measured on an ECG include PR-interval QRS interval (also called an 'QRS' duration), QT interval and 'RR' interval.

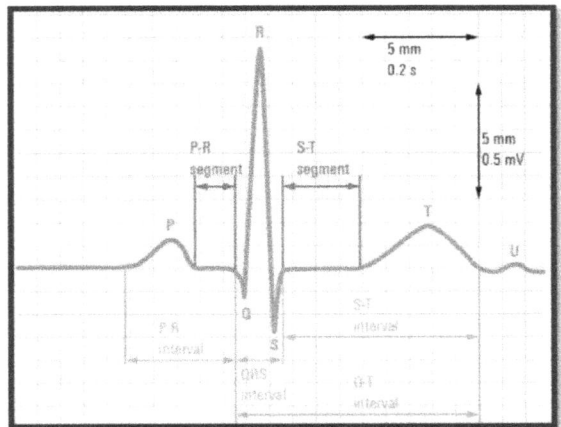

Segment:- The length between two specific points on an ECG that are supposed to be at the baseline amplitude (not negative or positive) the segments on an ECG include the PR-segment, ST- segment and TP segment.

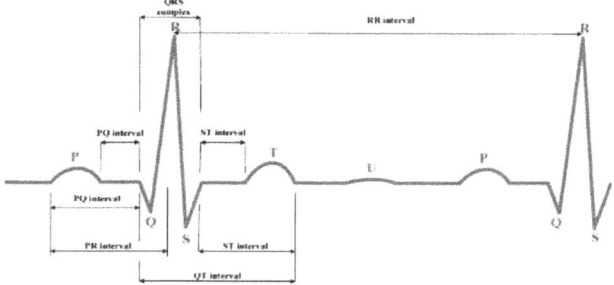

Complex: - The combination of multiple waves grouped together. The only main complex on an ECG is "QRS" complex.

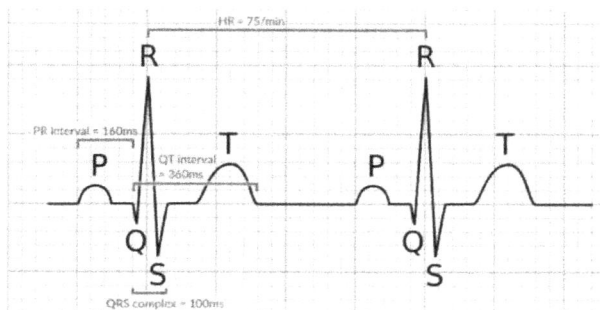

Point:- There is only one point on an ECG termed as "J" point which is where the QRS complex ends and the ST- segment begins.

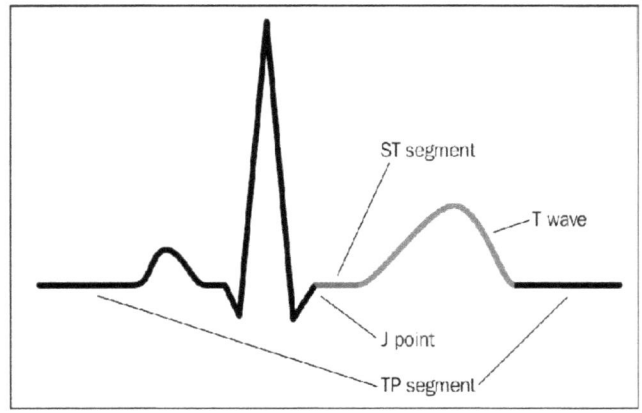

The main point of the ECG contains a 'P'-wave, QRS complex and 'T'-wave.

P-Wave

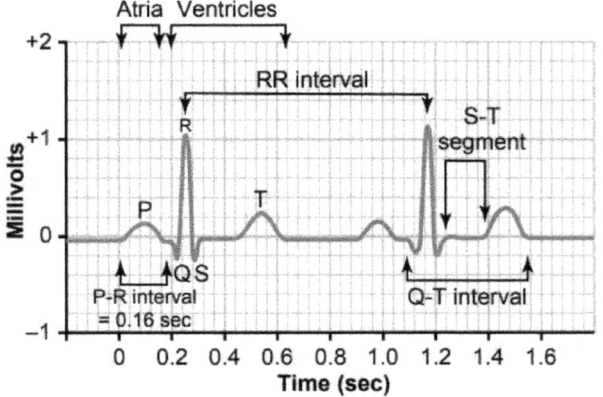

"P"- Waves

P Waves :- 'P'-wave indicates atrial depolarization the 'P'-wave occurs when the sinus node , also known as the sinus – atrial node , creates an action potential that depolarizes the atria .

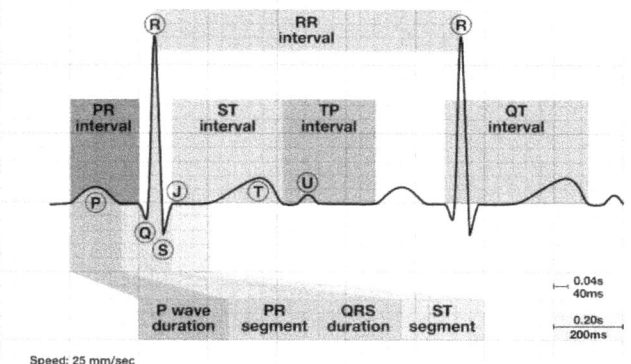

The 'P'-waves should be upright in lead II if the action potential is originating from the SA node. In this setting the ECG is said to demonstrate a normal sinus rhythm. As long as the atrial depolarization is able to spread through the atrial –ventricular (AV)node to the ventricles. Each 'P'-wave should be followed by 'QRS'-complex.

- 'P'-wave is the first positive deflection on the ECG AND represents atrial –depolarization.

- Duration <0.12s (<120ms or 3small squares).

Characteristics of Normal 'P'-wave

Morphology: -
- Smooth contour
- Monophasic in lead II
- Bi-phasic in V1.

Axis:-
- Normal 'P'-wave axis is between 0 degree. and +75degree.
- 'P'- waves should be upright in leads I and II, inverted in avR.

Duration :-
<0.12 s(<120 ms or 3 small squares)

Amplitude :-
- < 2.5 mm (0.25mv) in the limb leads.
- <1.5 mm (0.15mv) in pre-cordial leads.

The atrial wave form relationship to 'P'-wave.
1) The atrial depolarization proceeds sequentially from right to left with the right atrium activated before the left atrium.
2) The right and left atrial wave form summate to form the 'P'-wave.
3) The first 1/3 of the 'P'-wave corresponds to right atrial activation, the final 1/3 of the 'P'-wave

corresponds the left atrial activation, the middle 1/3 is a combination of two.

4) In most leads. (II) the eight and left atrial wave forms move in same direction, forming a monophasic 'P'-wave.

5) However in lead v1 the right and left atrial wave form move in opposite directions forming biphasic 'P'-wave with initial positive deflection corresponding to right atrial activation and the subsequent negative deflection denoting left atrial activation.

6) This separation of right and left atrial electrical forces in lead v1 means that abnormalities affecting each individual atrial waveform can be discerned in this lead. Elsewhere, the overall shape of 'P'-wave is used to infer the atrial abnormality.

Normal p-wave morphology-lead II.

- The right atrial depolarisation wave precedes that of the left atrium.
- The combined depolarisation wave, the 'P'-wave is less than 120 ms wide and less than 2.5 mm high.

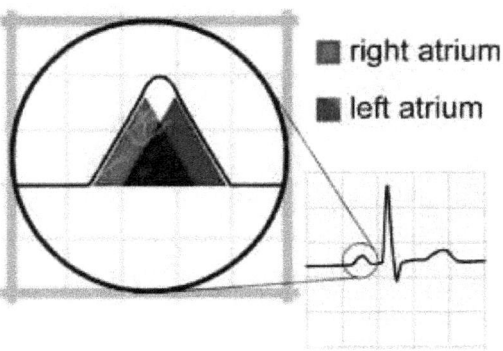

Normal morphology in lead v1

The 'P'-wave is typically biphasic in v1 with similar sizes of the positive and negative deflection.

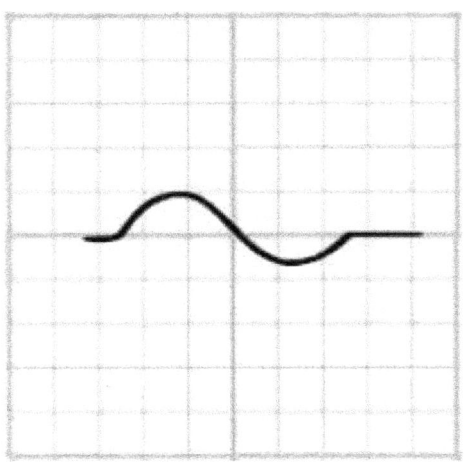

PR-Interval

- ✓ The PR-interval is the time from the onset of the 'P'-wave to the start of the QRS complex. It reflects conduction through the AV node.
- ✓ The normal PR-interval is between 120-200ms (0.12 - .20s) in duration (three to five small square).

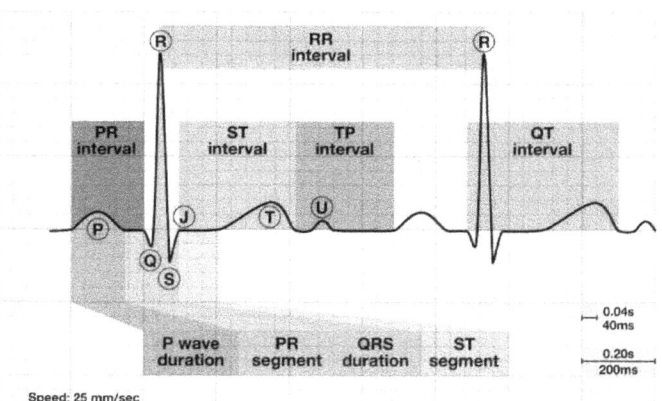

PR –Segment

The PR segment is the flat, usually isoelectric segment between the end of 'P'-wave and the start of the QRS complex.

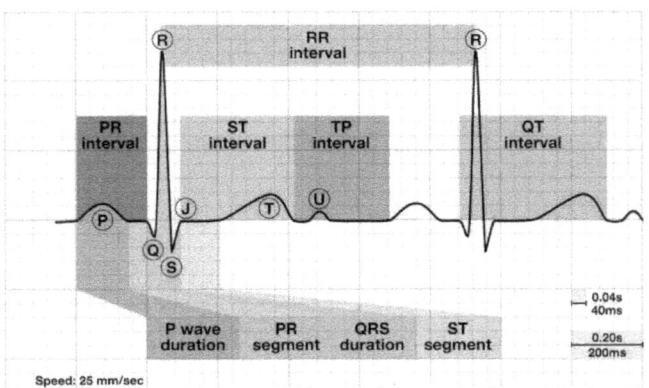

Q Wave

The 'Q'-wave is any negative deflection that proceeds an 'R'-wave.

- The 'Q'-wave represents the normal left to right depolarisation of the interventricular septum.
- Small septal 'Q'-wave are typically seen in the left sided leads (I, avL, v5 and v6).

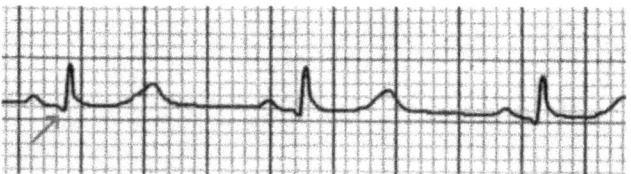

Q waves in different leads:-

- Small 'Q'-waves are normal in most leads.
- Deeper 'Q'-waves (>2mm) may be seen in leads III and avR as a normal variant.
- Under normal circumstances, 'Q'-waves are not seen in the right sided leads (v1 – v3).

QT – Interval

The QT-interval is the time from the start of 'QT'-wave to the end of the 'T'-wave.

It represents the time taken for the ventricular depolarisation and repolarisation, effectively the period of ventricular systole from ventricular iso-volumetric contraction to iso-volumetric relaxation.

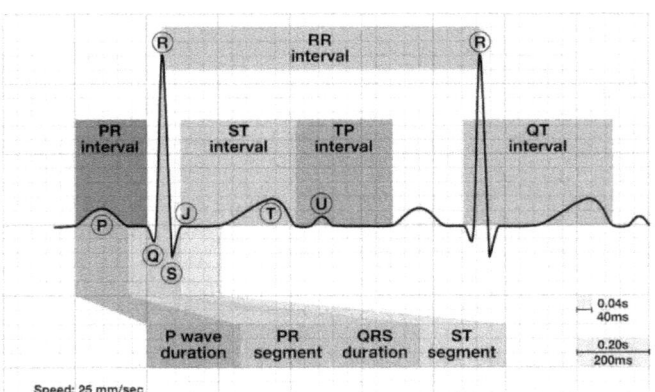

How to measure QT- interval:-

1) The QT-interval should be measured in either lead II or v5 –v6.
2) Several successive beats should be measured with maximum interval taken.
3) Large 'U' –waves (>1mm) that are fused to the 'T'-wave should be the included in the measurement.

4) Smaller 'U'-waves and those are separate from the 'T'-wave should be excluded.

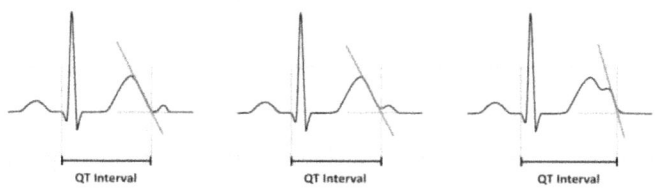

Intersection of T wave maximum slope with the isoelectric line

'J'- Point: -

- The J-point is the junction b/w the termination of the QRS-complex and the beginning of the ST segment.

- The 'J' (junction) point makes the end the QRS complex, and is often situated above the baseline, particularly in healthy young males.

On most ECG's the determination of the 'J'-point as a demarcation b/w the QRS and the start of the ST is clear.

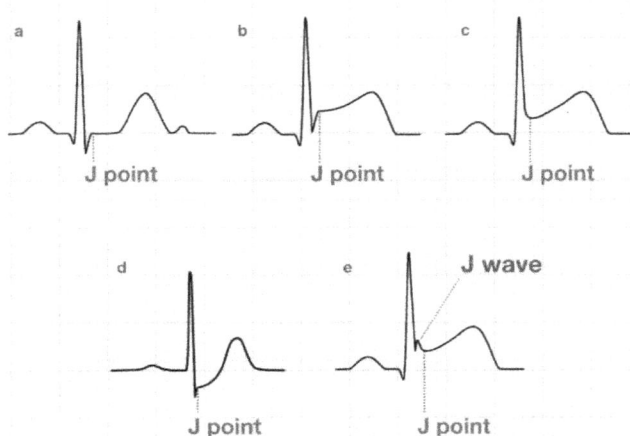

J point in a) normal; b) c) J point elevation; d) J point depression; e) with J wave (Osborn wave)

ST - Segment: -

- The ST-segment is the flat, isoelectric section of the ECG b/w the end of the 'S'-wave (the 'J'-point) and the beginning of the 'T'-wave.
- The ST-segment represents the interval b/w the ventricular depolarisation and repolarisation.

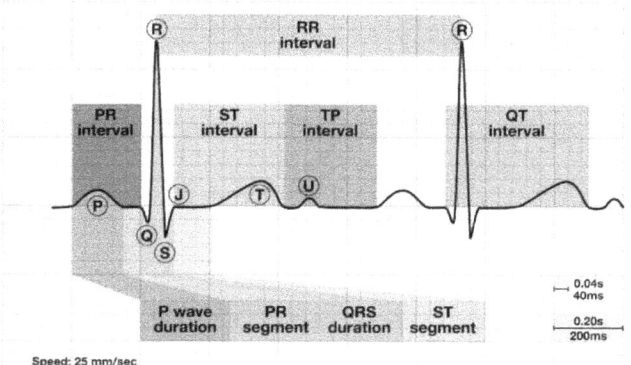

'R'-wave :-

The 'R'-wave is the first upward deflection after the 'P'-wave. The 'R'-wave represents early ventricular depolarisation.

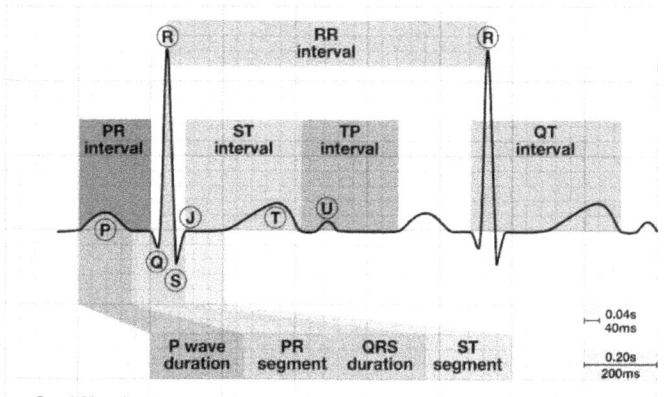

'T'-wave:-

The 'T'-wave is the positive deflection after each QRS complex. It represents ventricular repolarisation.

Characteristics of normal 'T'-wave.

- Upright in all leads except avR and v1.
- Amplitude <5mm in limb leads, <10mm in precordial leads (10mm in men, 8mm in women).

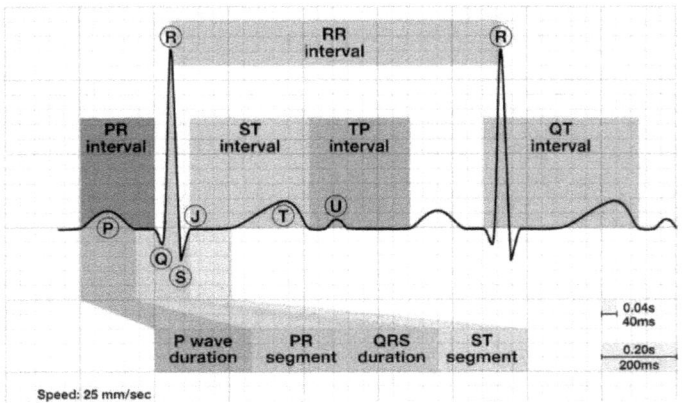

U-wave:-

➢ The U-wave is small (0.5mm) deflection immediately following the 'T'-wave.

- 'U'-wave is usually in the same direction on the 'T'-wave.
- 'U'-wave is best seen in leads v2 and v3.

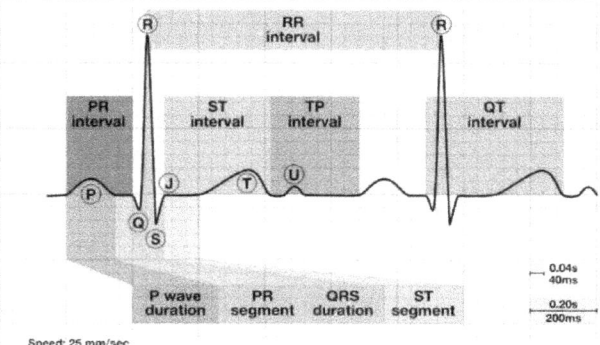

Source of the 'U'-wave.

The source of the 'T'-wave is unknown. Three common theories regarding its origin are: -

1) Delayed repolarisation of the 'U'-wave of purkinje fibres.
2) Prolonged repolarisation of the mid-myocardial "M-cells".
3) After potentials resulting from mechanical forces in the ventricular wall.

Features of normal 'U'-waves: -

- The 'U'-wave normally goes in the same direction on the 'T'- wave.
- 'U'-wave size is inversely proportional to the heart rate the 'U'-wave grows bigger as the heart rate slow down.
- 'U'-wave generally become visible when the heart rate falls below 65 bpm.

- The voltage of 'U'-wave is normally <25% of the 'T'-wave voltage: disproportionally large 'U'-waves are abnormal.
- Maximum normal amplitude of 'U'-wave is 1-2mm.

Bundle Branch Block

Bundle branch block: - It is a condition in which there a delay or blockage along the pathway that electrical impulses travel to make your heart beat. It sometimes makes it harder for your heart to pump blood efficiently through your body.

The delay or blockage can occur on the pathway that sends electrical impulses either to the left or the right side of the bottom chambers (ventricles) of the heart.

Symptoms: -

In most people, bundle branch block doesn't cause symptoms. Some people with the condition don't know have a bundle branch block.

Signs and symptom in people who have then might include: -

1) Fainting (syncope)
2) Feeling as if you're going to faint.

Causes: -

The causes for bundle branch blocks can differ depending on whether the left or right bundle branch is affected. It's also possible that this condition can occur without a known cause.

Causes can include: -
1) **Left bundle branch block: -**
   - Heart attacks [myocardial infarction]
   - Thickened, stiffened or weakened heart muscle [cardiomyopathy]
   - A viral or bacterial infection of the heart muscle (myocarditis)
   - High blood pressure (hypertension)
2) **Right bundle branch block:-**
   - Increasing age: - Bundle branch block is more common in older adults than in younger people.
   - Underlying health problems: - Having high blood pressure or heart disease increases your risk of having bundle branch block.

Left Bundle Branch Block

Definition:- LBBB a delay or blockage of electrical impulses to the left side of the heart.

Causes:-
1) Aortic stenosis
2) Ischaemic heart disease
3) Hypertension
4) Dilated cardiomyopathy
5) Anterior M.I
6) Primary degenerative disease of the conducting system.
7) Hyperkalaemia
8) Digoxin toxicity.

- Normally the septum is activated from left to right producing small 'Q'-waves in the lateral leads.

- In LBBB, the normal direction of septal depolarisation is reversed, as the impulses spread first to the RV via the right bundle branch and then to LV via the septum.

- This sequences of activation extends the QRS duration to >120ms and eliminates the normal septal 'Q'-waves in the lateral leads.

- The overall direction of depolarisation produces the tall 'R'-waves in the lateral leads (I, v5-v6) and deep 'S'-wave in right precordial leads (v1-v3) and usually leads to left axis deviation.
- As the ventricles are activated sequentially rather than simultaneously, this produces the broad ('M'-shape) 'R'-wave in lateral leads.

ECG criteria:-
1) 1QRS complex duration of >120ms.
2) Dominant 'S'-wave in v1
3) Broad monophasic 'R'-wave in lateral leads [I, avL, v5-v6]
4) Absence of 'Q'-waves in lateral leads [I, v5-v6]
5) Prolonged 'R'-wave peak time >60ms in pre-cordial leads [v5-v6].

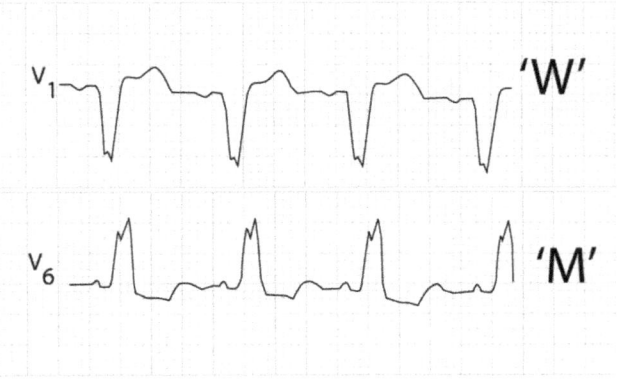

Associated features: -
- Appropriate discordances: The ST segments and 'T'-waves always go in the opposite direction to the main vector of QRS complex.

- Poor 'r'-wave progression in the chest leads.
- Left axis deviation.

ECG QRS morphology: -

QRS morphology in the lateral leads.

The 'R'-wave in the lateral leads may be either: -

1) 'M'-shaped
2) Notched
3) Mono-phasic
4) RS-complex.

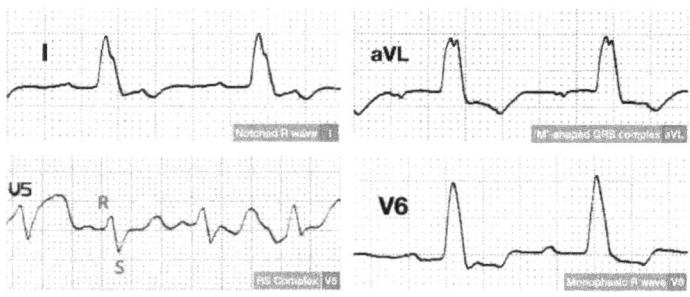

QRS morphology in v1

The QRS complex in v1 may be either: -

1) 1rS complex (small 'R'-wave, deep 'S'-wave)
2) QS complex (deep Q/S wave with no preceding 'R'-wave).

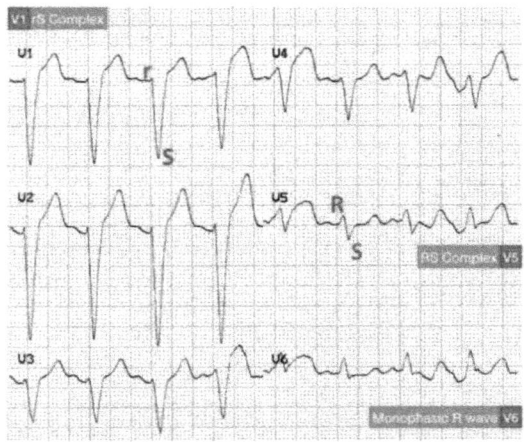

Incomplete LBBB

Incomplete LBBB is diagnosed when typical LBBB morphology associated with a QRS duration <120ms.

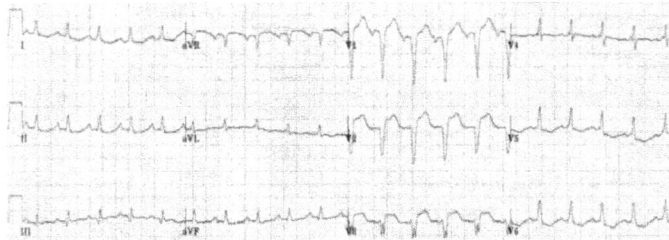

Right Bundle Branch Block

Definition: - RBBB is a Blockage of electrical impulses to the heart right ventricle.

Causes: -
1) Right ventricular hypertrophy
2) Pulmonary embolus
3) Ischaemic heart disease
4) Rheumatic heart disease
5) Cardiomyopathy
6) Degenerative disease of conduction system
7) Congenital heart disease.

Symptoms: -

RBBB doesn't always cause symptoms. Infact some people have it for years and never know. However, a delay in the arrival of electrical impulses to the heart's right ventricle can cause.

1) Syncope [which is fainting due to unusual heart rhythms that affect blood pressure]
2) Pre-syncope.

RBBB

In RBBB, activation of the right ventricle is delayed as depolarisation has to spread across the septum from the left ventricle.

- The left ventricle is activated normally, meaning that the early part of QRS complex is unchanged.
- The delayed right ventricular activation produces a secondary 'R'-wave in the right pre-cordial leads [v1 – v3] and a wide, slurred 'S'-wave in lateral leads.
- Delayed activation of the right ventricle also gives rise to secondary repolarisation. Abnormalities with the ST- depression and 'T'-wave inversion in the right pre-cordial leads.
- In isolated RBBB the cardiac axis is unchanged as left ventricular activation proceeds normally via the bundle branch.

ECG changes in RBBB: -

Diagnostic criteria
1) Broad QRS >120ms.
2) RSR1 pattern in v1-v3 ('M'-shaped, QRS complex)
3) Wide, slurred 'S'-wave inlateral leads (I, avL, v5-v6)

Rhythms

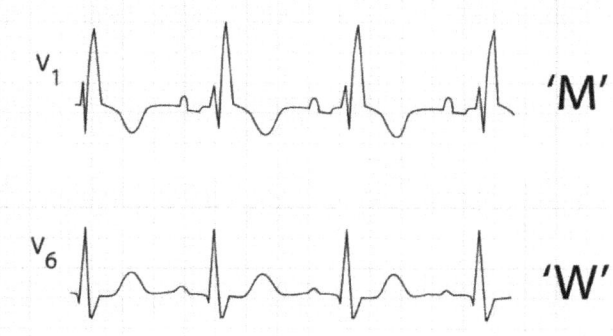

Associated features: -

ST-depression and 'T'-wave inversion in right precordial leads (v1 –v3).

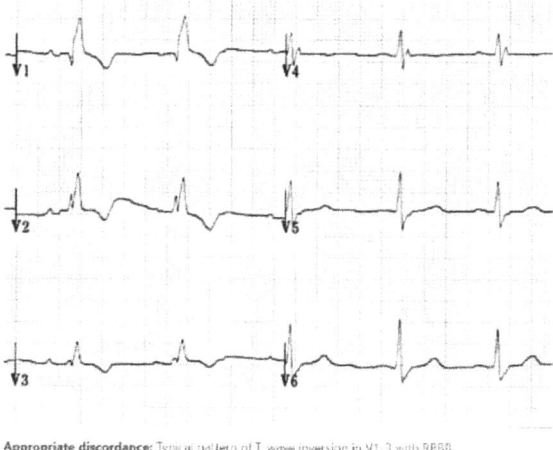

Appropriate discordance: Typical pattern of T wave inversion in V1-3 with RBBB

Incomplete RBBB

1) Incomplete RBBB is defined as an RSR1 pattern in v1-v3 with QRS duration <120ms.

2) It is a normal variant, commonly seen in children.

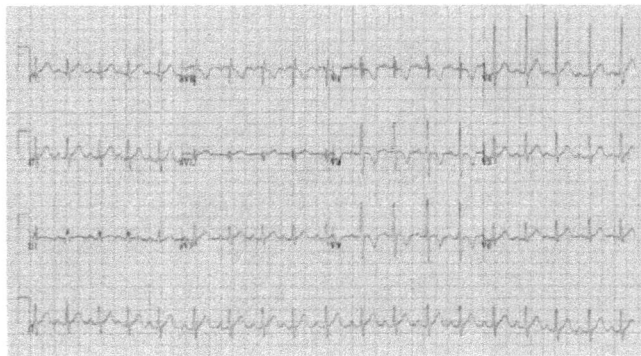

Fascicular Blocks

What are fascicular blocks?

Fascicular block involves the anterior or posterior fascicle of the left bundle branch.

Causes: -
1) Some LAFB are a result of age-related conduction system disease.
2) Others are indeed, from structural heart problems these can include coronary artery disease, prior myocardial infraction.
3) Left ventricular hypertrophy from hypertensive heart disease.
4) Cardiomyopathies.
5) Valvular heart disease.

Types of fascicular block

They are divided into two types
1) Left anterior fascicular block [LAFB]
2) Left posterior fascicular block [LPFB]

Left anterior fascicular block [LAFB]

In LAFB, impulses are conducted to the left ventricle via the left posterior fascicle, which insects into the inferoseptal wall of the left ventricle along its endocardial surface.

- In reaching the left ventricle, the initial electrical vector is therefore directed downwards and rightwards, producing small 'R'-waves in the interior leads [II, III, avF] and small 'Q'-waves in the left sided leads. (I, avL)
- The major waves of depolarisation then spreads, in an upwards and leftwards direction, producing large positive voltages [Tall 'R'-wave] in the left sided leads and large negative voltages [deep 'S'-wave] in the interior leads.
- This process takes about 20milliseconds longer than simultaneous condition via both fascicles, resulting ina slight widening of the QRS.
- The impulse reaches the left-sided leads later thannormal resulting ina increased 'R'- wave peak time in avL.

ECG criteria of LAFB.

1) Left axis deviation [usually b/w -45 and -90degrees].
2) Small 'Q'-waves with tall 'R'-waves ['qR complex'] in leads I and avL
3) Small 'R'- waves with deep 'S'-waves ['rs complex'] in leads II, III, avF.
4) QRS duration normal or slightly prolonged [80-110ms]
5) Prolonged 'R'-wave peak time in avL >45ms.

6) Increased QRS voltage in the limb leads.

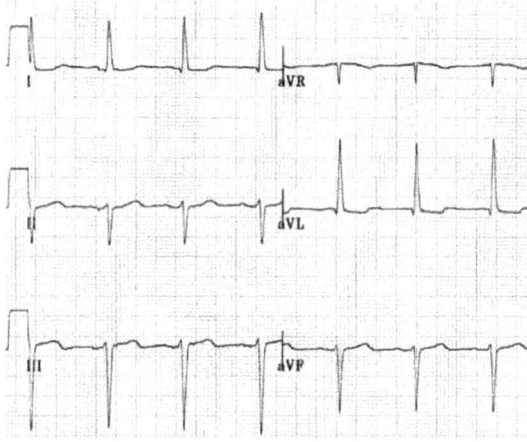

ECG Morphology

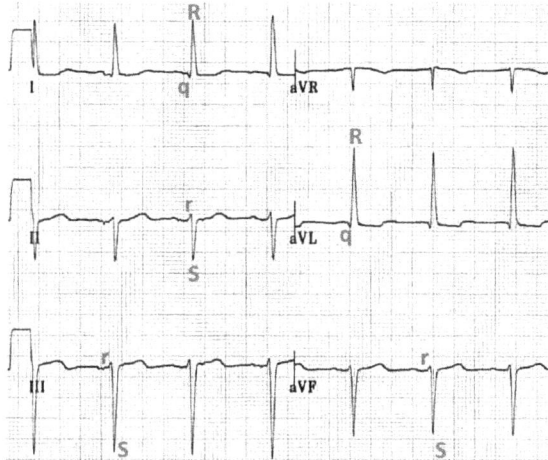

qR complexes in lateral limb leads, and **rS complexes** in inferior leads

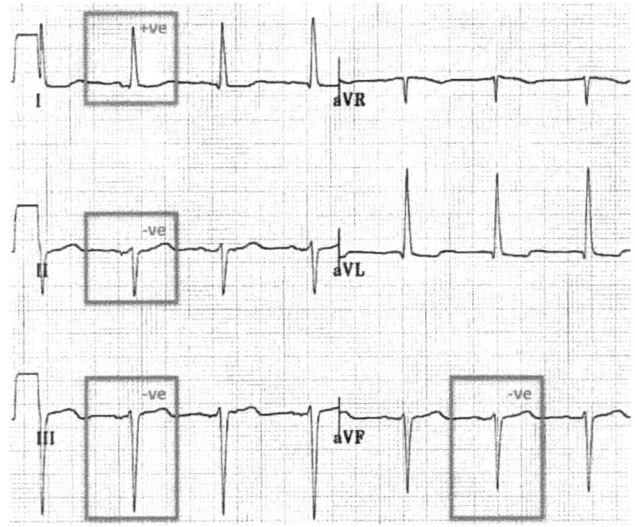

Left Axis Deviation (LAD)

- Leads I and aVL are *POSITIVE;*
- Leads II, III and aVF are *NEGATIVE*

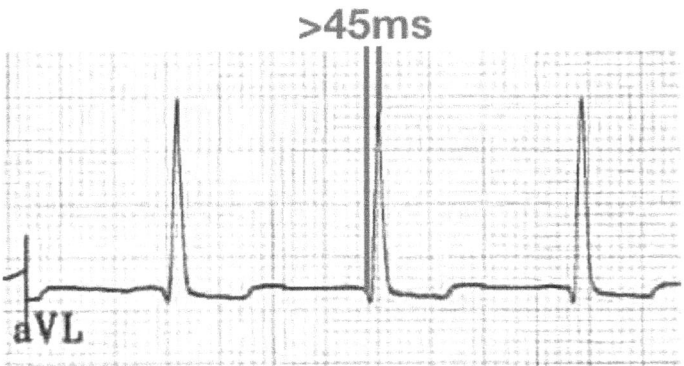

Prolonged R-wave peak time

- Prolonged R-wave peak time (= the time from onset of the QRS to the peak of the R wave) in aVL > 45 ms

Left Posterior Fascicular Block [LPFB]

In LPFB impulses are conducted to the left ventricle via the left anterior fascicle, which inserts into the upper, lateral wall of the left ventricle along the endocardia surface.

- On reaching the ventricle, the initial electrical vector is therefore directed upwards and leftwards causing small 'R'-waves in lateral leads [I and avL] and small 'Q'-waves in interior leads [II, III, avF].

- The major wave of depolarisation then spreads along the free LV wall ina downward and rightward direction, producing large positive voltages [Tall 'R'-waves] in the interior leads and large negative voltages [deep 'S'-waves] in the lateral leads.

- This process takes up to 20ms longer than simultaneous conduction via both fascicles, resulting in a slight widening of the QRS.

- The impulses reaches the interior leads later than normal, resulting in increased 'R'-wave peak time in avF.

ECG of LPFB :-

1) Right axis deviation [> +90degrees]
2) Small 'R'-waves with deep 'S'-waves [rS complex]
3) Small 'Q'-waves with tall 'R'-waves [qRcomplex]
4) QRS duration normal or slightly prolonged [80-110ms].
5) Prolonged 'R'-wave peak time in avF.
6) Measured QRS-voltage in limb leads.
7) No evidence of right ventricular hypertrophy.
8) No evidence of any other cause for right axis deviation.

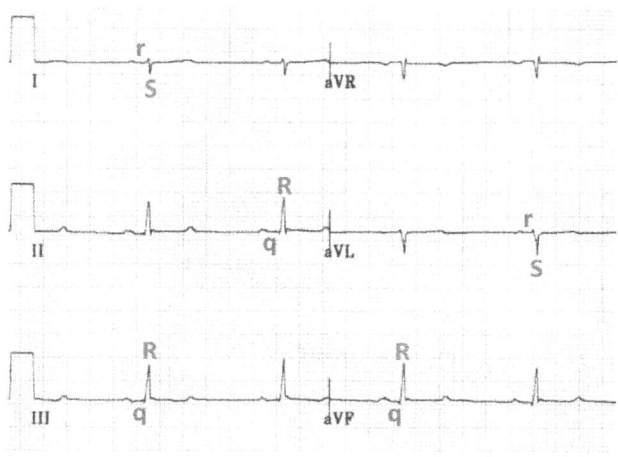

Left Posterior Fascicular Block (LPFB)

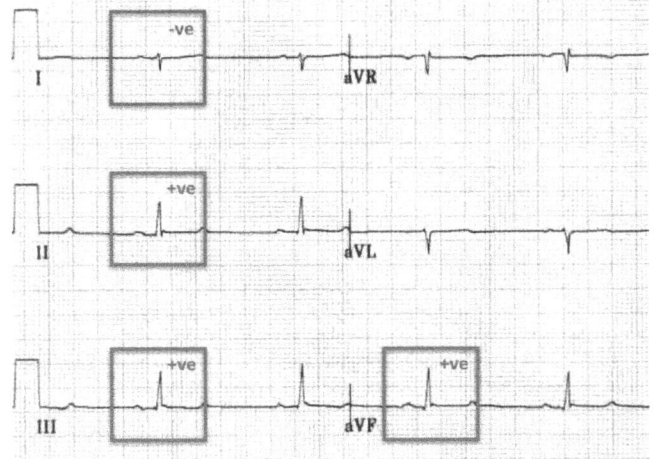

Right Axis Deviation (RAD)

Leads II, III and aVF are POSITIVE;

Leads I and aVL are NEGATIVE

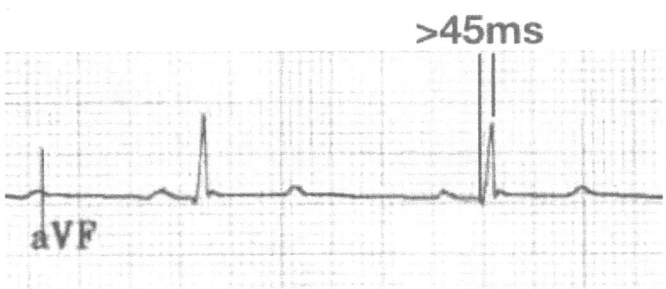

Prolonged R-wave peak time

R-wave peak time: Time from onset of the QRS to the peak of the R wave in aVF > 45 ms

Interventricular Conduction Delay (QRS-Widening)

Definition of QRS widening: -

QRS duration >100ms in the presence of supraventricular rhythm. Most commonly due to bundle branch block or left ventricular hypertrophy.

The most important life-threatening cause of QRS widening are:-

1) Hyperkalaemia
2) Tricyclic anti-depressant poisoning.

Causes:- Fascicular and bundle branch blocks.

1) Left anterior fascicular block.
2) Left posterior fascicular block.
3) Left bundle branch block.
4) Right bundle branch block.
5) Bi fascicular block.
6) Tri fascicular block.

Ventricular hypertrophy and dilatation
1) Left ventricular hypertrophy
2) Right ventricular hypertrophy
3) Bi-ventricular enlargement
4) Dilated cardiomyopathy

Electrolyte abnormalities: -
1) Hyperkalaemia

Toxins: -
1) Sodium-channel blocks toxicity [eg. TCA overdose] wide QRS plus positive 'R'- wave in avR.

Bi-Fascicular Block

Bi-fascicular block is the combination of RBBB with either LAFB or LPFB.

- Conduction to the ventricles is via the single remaining fascicle.
- The ECG show typical features of RBBB plus either left or right axis deviation.
- RBBB + LAFB is the most common of the two patterns.
- Bi-fascicular block is a sign of extensive conducting system disease, although the risk progressing to complete heart block is thought to be relatively low.

Causes: -
1) Ischaemic heart disease [40-60%cases]
2) Hypertension (20-25%)
3) Aortic stenosis
4) Anterior MI
5) Congenital heart disease
6) Hyperkalaemia.

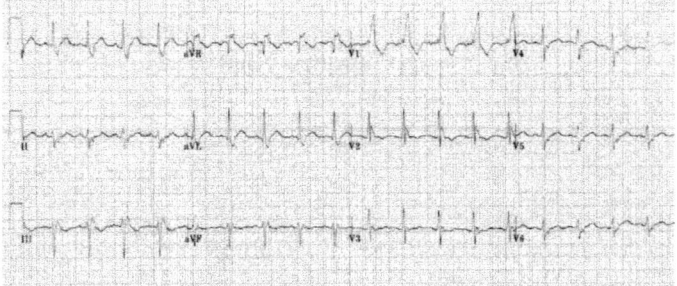

Tri-Fascicular Block

Definition of tri-fascicular block:-

Tri-fascicular block [TFB] refers to the presence of conducting disease in all three fascicles.

1) Right bundle branch
2) Left anterior fascicle [LAF]
3) Left posterior fascicle [LPF]

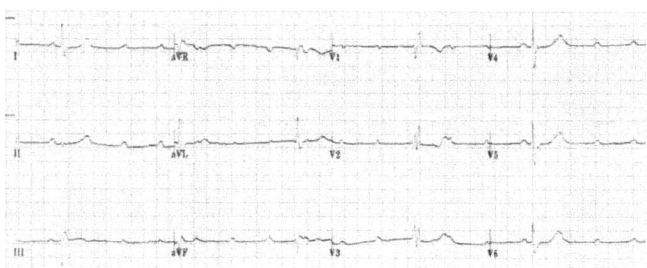

True Trifascicular Block:

- Right bundle branch block
- Left axis deviation (Left anterior fascicular block)
- Third degree heart block

Incomplete vs complete TFB.

Tri-fascicular block can be incomplete or complete depending on whether all the three fascicles have completely failed or not.

Incomplete Tri-fascicular block.

Incomplete Tri-fascicular block can be inferred from one of two electrocardiographic patterns.

1) Fixed blocks of two fascicles, with delayed conduction in the remaining fascicles. [i.e is 1st or 2nd degree AV block].
2) Fixed block of one fascicle [i,e RBBB] with intermittent failure of the other two fascicles [i,e alternating LAFB/LPFB]

Complete Tri-fascicular block

- Complete Tri-fascicular block produces 3rd degree AV block with features of Bi-fascicular block.
- This is because the escape rhythm usually arises from the region of either the left anterior or left posterior fascicle producing QRS complexes with appearances, of RBBB plus either LPFB or LAFB respectively.

Patterns of TFB:-
Incomplete TFB

1) Bi-fascicular block + 1st degree AV block [most common]
2) Bi-fascicular block+ 2nd degree AV block

3) RBBB + alternating LAFB/LPFB.

Complete TFB: -
1) Bi-fascicular block + 3rd degree AV block.

Causes:-
1) Ischaemic heart disease
2) Hypertension
3) Aortic stenosis
4) Anterior MI
5) Primary regenerative disease of the conducting system.
6) Congenital heart disease
7) Hyperkalaemia
8) Digoxin toxicity.

First Degree Heart Block

PR interval >120ms [five small squares]

- Marked first degree block if PR interval >300ms
- Does not cause haemodynamic disturbance.
- No specific treatment is required.

Causes of 1st Degree Heart Block

1) Increased vagal tone
2) Athletic training
3) Interior MI
4) Mitral valve surgery
5) Myocarditis
6) Electrolyte disturbance
7) AV nodal blocking drugs

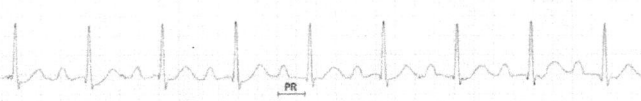

2nd Degree, Mobitz I [Wenckbach Phenomenon]

AV Block:- 2nd degree AV block ,mobitz I [wenckbach] in a non-conducted 'P'-wave [compare to mobitz II]

- PR normal is longest immediately before the dropped beat.
- The PR interval is the shortest immediately after the dropped beat.

Other features of 2nd degree, mobitz I :-

1) The P-P interval remains constant.
2) The greatest increase in PR interval duration is typically b/w the 1st and 2nd beats of cycle.
3) The R-R interval progressively shortens with each beat of the cycle.
4) The wenckebach pattern tends to repeat in P:QRS groups with ratio of 3:2 , 4:3 OR 5:4

Causes :-
1) Drugs : beta blockers
2) Increased vagal tone
3) Interior MI
4) Myocarditis
5) Mitral valve repair
6) Tetralogy of fallot repair

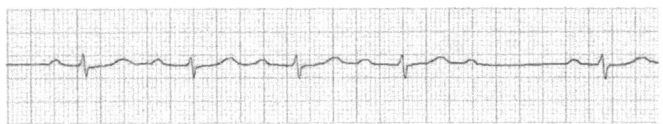

AV block: 2nd degree, Mobitz type I

AV Block :- 2nd Degree, Mobitz II

Intermittent non-conducted 'P'-waves without progressive prolongation of PR interval.

- The PR interval in the conducted beats remain constant.
- 'P'-waves 'march through' at a constant rate.
- The 'R-R' interval surrounding the dropped beats is an eaxact multiple of the precending RR interval.

Causes of mobitz II :-
1) Anterior M.I [due to septal infarction with necrosis of bundle branches]
2) Idiopathic fibrosis of the conducting system
3) Cardiac surgeries [M.V repair]
4) Inflammatory condition [Rheumatic fever]

5) Autoimmune
6) Infiltrative myocardial disease
7) Hyperkalaemia
8) Drugs :- beta blockers.

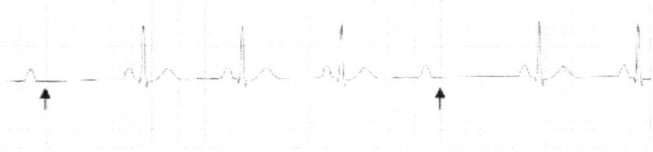

Complete Heart Block

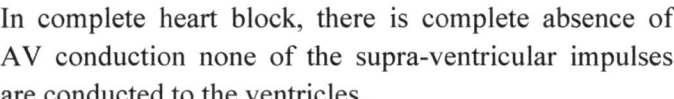

In complete heart block, there is complete absence of AV conduction none of the supra-ventricular impulses are conducted to the ventricles.

Perfusing rhythm is maintained by a junctional or ventricular escape rhythm. Alternatively, the patient may suffer ventricular standstill leading to syncope.

Causes of complete heart block: -

The causes are the same as for mobitz I and mobitz II-degree heart block. The most important aetiologies are:-

- Inferior myocardial infarction
- AV-nodal blocking drugs
- Idiopathic degeneration of conducting system.

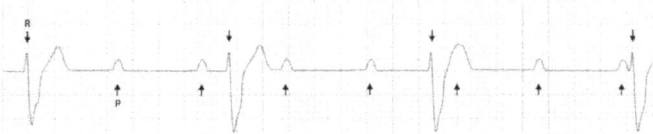

Atrial Enlargement

Atrial enlargement refers to an enlarged atrium that is right atrium and left atrium.

They are divided into two types.

1) Left Atrial Enlargement
2) Right Atrial Enlargement.

1) **Left Atrial Enlargement:-** It refers to enlargement of the left Atrium of heart and is form of cardiomegaly.

Signs and Symptoms:-
1) Chest pain
2) Breathing problems, including shortens of breath and coughing
3) Extreme fatigue
4) Abnormal heart beat
5) Fainting.

Causes:-
1) High blood pressure
2) Atrial fibrillation
3) Mitral valve dysfunction
4) Left ventricle problems
5) Left Atrial pressures

6) Elevated left Atrial volume

ECG :- LAE produces a broad, bifid 'P'-wave in lead II [P-mitrale] and enlarges the terminal negative portion of 'P'-wave in lead v1.

	II	V1
Normal	⋀	⌢
RAE	⋀	⋀
LAE	⋔	⌢⌣
RAE + LAE	⋔	⋀⌣

'P'-wave in lead II

- Bifid 'P'-wave with >40ms b/w the two peaks.
- Total 'P'-wave duration >110ms.

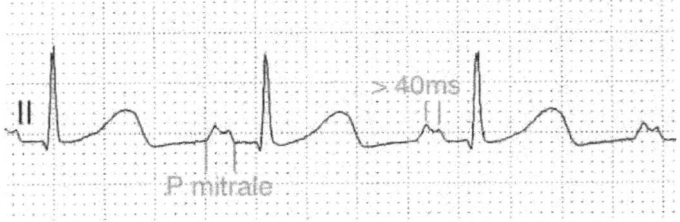

Broad (>110ms), bifid P wave in lead II (P mitrale) with > 40ms between the peaks

'P'-wave in v1

- Bi-phasic 'P'-wave with terminal negative portion >40mm.
- Bi-phasic 'P'-wave with terminal negative portion >1mm deep.

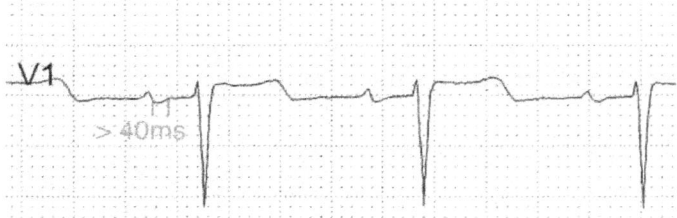

P wave terminal portion > 40 ms duration in V1

2) Right Atrial Enlargement

Right Atrial Enlargement:-

Right atrial enlargement refers to dilation of right atrium.

Symptoms :-

1) Shortness of breath (28% of cases)
2) Palpitation (17% of cases)
3) Arrhythmias (12%)
4) In rare cases, right heart failure.
5) Extreme tiredness

Causes :-
1) Congenital heart disease
2) Primary pulmonary hypertension
3) Chronic lung disease
4) Tricuspid stenosis.
5) Pulmonary stenosis.

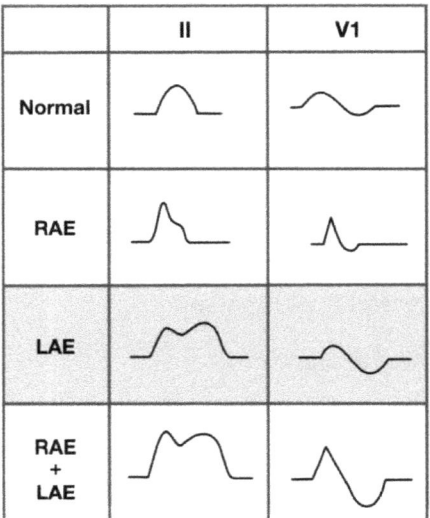

ECG in Right Atrial Enlargement:-

Right atrial enlargement produces a peaked 'P'-wave_'P'-pulmonale with amplitude.

- >2.5mm in the inferior leads [II, III, avF]
- >1.5mm in v1 and v2.

Rhythms

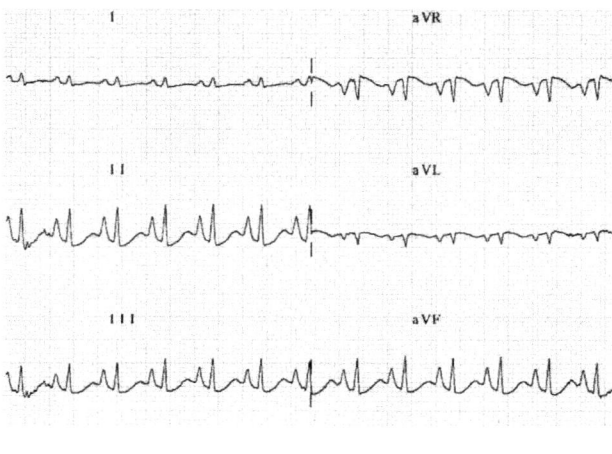

Cardiac Hypertrophy

Cardiac hypertrophy is the abnormal enlargement or thickening of the heart muscle, resulting from increase incardiomyocyte size and changes in heart muscle components such as extracellular matrix.

Symptoms :-
1) Shortness of breath
2) Fatigue
3) Chest pain
4) Palpitations
5) Dizziness.

Causes: -
1) High blood pressure
2) Aortic valve stenosis
3) Hypertrophy cardiomyopathy.

Types: - Cardiac hypertrophy divided into two types
1) Right ventricular hypertrophy
2) Left ventricular hypertrophy

Left Ventricular Hypertrophy
LVH

- The left ventricle hypertrophies in response to pressure overload secondary to condition such as aortic stenosis and hypertensions.

- This results in increased 'R'-wave amplitude in the left sided ECG leads [I, avL and v4-v6] and increased 'S'-wave depth in the right sided leads [III, avR, v1-v3]

- The thickened LV wall leads to prolonged depolarisation [increased 'R'-wave peak time] and delayed repolarisation [ST and T-wave abnormalities] in the lateral leads.

Criteria for diagnosing LVH

- There are numerous criteria for diagnosing LVH source of which are summarised below.

- Most commonly used are the "SOKOLOV-LYON" criteria ['S-wave depth in v1 + Tall 'R'-wave height in v5-v6> 35mm]

- Voltage criteria must be accompanied by non-voltage criteria to be considered diagnostic of LVH.

Voltage criteria
Limb leads:-

- 'R'-wave in lead I + 'S'-wave in lead III >25mm
- 'R'-wave in avL >11mm
- 'R'-wave in avF >20mm

- 'S'-wave in avR > 14mm

Precordial leads
- 'R'-wave in v4, v5 or v6 > 26mm
- 'R'-wave in v5 or v6 plus 'S'-wave in v1 > 35mm
- Largest 'R'-wave plus largest 'S'-wave in pre-cordial leads > 45mm.

Additional ECG changes in LVH
- Left axis deviation
- Left atrial enlargement
- ST-elevation in right pre-cordial leads v1-v3
- Prominent 'U'-waves.

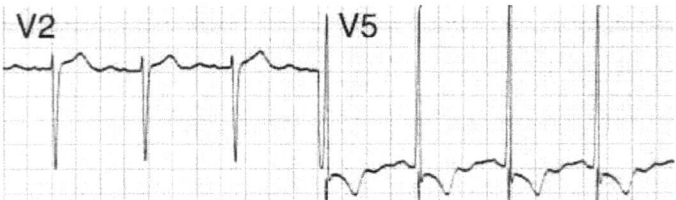

LVH by voltage criteria: S wave in V2 + R wave in V5 > 35 mm

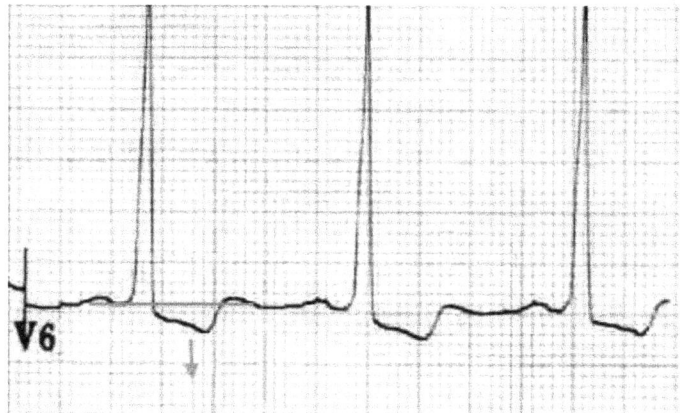

LV strain pattern: ST depression and T wave inversion in the lateral leads

Causes of LVH: -
1) Hypertension
2) Aortic stenosis
3) Aortic regurgitation
4) Mitral regurgitation
5) Coarctation of aorta.

Symptoms of LVH: -
1) Chest pain
2) Dizziness
3) Shortness in breathing
4) Fluttering

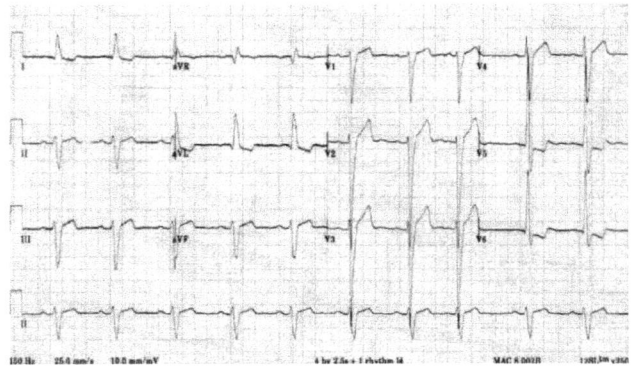

Left ventricular hypertrophy (LVH):

- Markedly increased LV voltages: huge precordial R and S waves that overlap with the adjacent leads (SV2 + RV6 >> 35 mm).
- R-wave peak time > 50 ms in V5-6 with associated QRS broadening.
- LV strain pattern with ST depression and T-wave inversions in I, aVL and V5-6.
- ST elevation in V1-3.
- Prominent U waves in V1-3.
- Left axis deviation.

Right Ventricular Hypertrophy

RVH
Causes :-
1) Pulmonary hypertension
2) Mitral stenosis
3) Pulmonary embolism
4) Chronic lung disease
5) Arrhythmogenic right ventricular cardiomyopathy.

Symptoms :-
1) Swelling in ankles, legs, feet
2) Fatigue
3) Chest pain
4) Shortness of breath

ECG features :-
- Right axis deviation of +110degree or more.
- Dominant 'R'-wave in v1 (>7mm Tall or R/S ratio >1)
- Dominant 'S'-wave in v5 or v6 (>7mm deep or R/S ratio <1)
- QRS duration <120ms.

Supporting criteria

- Right atrial enlargement
- Right ventricular strain pattern
- Strain pattern = ST depression/ 'T'-wave inversion in (v1-4) and in (II, III, avF) inferior leads
- Deep 'S'-waves in lateral leads [I, avL, v5-v6]

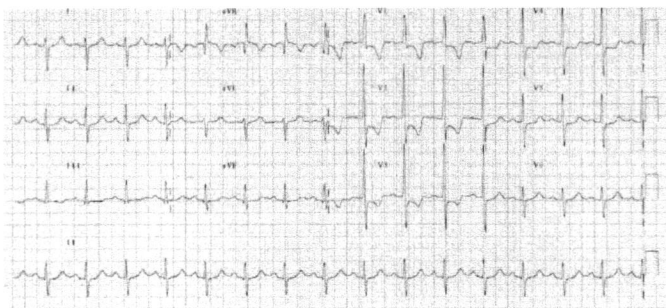

Typical appearance of RVH:

- Right axis deviation (+150 degrees).
- Dominant R wave in V1 (> 7 mm tall; R/S ratio > 1)
- Dominant S wave in V6 (> 7 mm deep; R/S ratio < 1).
- Right ventricular strain pattern with ST depression and T-wave inversion in V1-4.

Cardiomyopathy

Cardiomyopathy:- It is a disease of heart muscle that makes it harder for your heart to pump blood to the rest of your body.

Cardiomyopathy are further divided into three types
1) Dilated
2) Hypertrophic
3) Restrictive.

Symptoms :-
1) Breathlessness with exertion or rest
2) Swelling of the legs
3) Cough while lying down
4) Fatigue
5) Dizziness

Causes :-
1) Long term high blood pressure
2) Chronic rapid heart rate
3) Heart valve problems
4) Heart tissue change from heart attack
5) Pregnancy complications.

Dilated Cardiomyopathy (DCM)

Dilated cardiomyopathy is a myocardial disease characterised by ventricular dilatation and global myocardial dysfunction [Ejection fraction <40%]

Types :- Ischaemic and Non- ischaemic

Causes :-

1) **Ischaemic:-** DCM commonly occurs following massive anterior STEMI due to extensive myocardial necrosis and loss of contractility

2) **Non-ischaemic :-**
    3) Most cases are idiopathic
    4) Up to 25% are familial

Symptoms :-

1) Fatigue

2) Shortness of breath(dyspnea) when you're active or lying down

3) Reduced ability to exercise

4) Swelling (edema) in your legs, ankles and feet.

5) Swelling of your abdomen due to fluid buildup (ascites)

6) Chest pain

7) Extra or unusual sounds heard when your heart beats (heart murmurs)

ECG :-

1) Most common ECG abnormalities are those associated with atrial and ventricular hypertrophy typically, left sided changes are seen but there may be signs of bi-atrial or bi-ventricular hypertrophy.

2) Inter-ventricular conduction delay [LBBB] occur due to cardiac dilatation.

3) Diffuse myocardial fibrosis may lead to reduced voltage QRS complexes, particularly in the limb leads. There may be a discrepancy of QRS voltages with signs of hypertrophy in v4-v6 and relatively low voltages in limb leads.

4) Abnormal 'Q'-waves are most often seen in leads in v1 to v4.

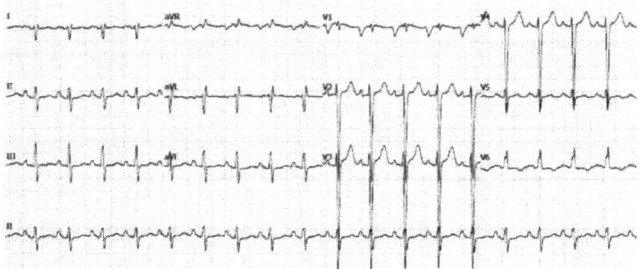

Ischaemic dilated cardiomyopathy:

- There is marked LVH (S wave in V2 > 35 mm) with dominant S waves in V1-4
- Right axis deviation suggests associated right ventricular hypertrophy (i.e. biventricular enlargement)
- There is evidence of left atrial enlargement (deep, wide terminal portion of the P wave in V1)
- There are peaked P waves in lead II suggestive of right atrial hypertrophy (not quite 2.5mm in height)

Common ECG associations with DCM

1) Left atrial enlargement
2) Bi-atrial enlargement
3) Left ventricular hypertrophy
4) Left bundle branch block
5) Left axis deviation
6) Ventricular ectopics.

Hypertrophy Cardiomyopathy [HCM]

HCM is one of the most common inherited cardiac disorders and is the number one cause of sudden cardiac death in young athletes.

Causes :-

1) Gene mutation
2) High blood pressure
3) Aging

Symptoms :-

1) Chest pain, especially during exercise
2) Fainting, especially during or just after exercise or exertion
3) Heart murmur, which a doctor might detect while listening to your heart
4) Sensation of rapid, fluttering or pounding heartbeats (palpitations)
5) Shortness of breath, especially during exercise.

ECG features:-
1) Left ventricular hypertrophy results in increased pre-cordial voltages and non-specific ST segment and 'T'-wave abnormalities.
2) Asymmetrical septal hypertrophic produces deep, narrow ["Dagger-like"] 'Q-wave' in the lateral [v5-v6, I,avL] and inferior [II, III, avF] leads. These may mimic prior myocardial infraction, although the 'Q'-wave morphology is different, Infraction 'Q'-wave are typically >40ms duration while septal 'Q'-wave in HCM are <40ms
3) Left ventricular diastolic dysfunction may lead to compensatory left atrial hypertrophy with signs of left atrial enlargement. "P-mitrale" on ECG
4) Atrial fibrillation
5) Supra-ventricular tachycardias.

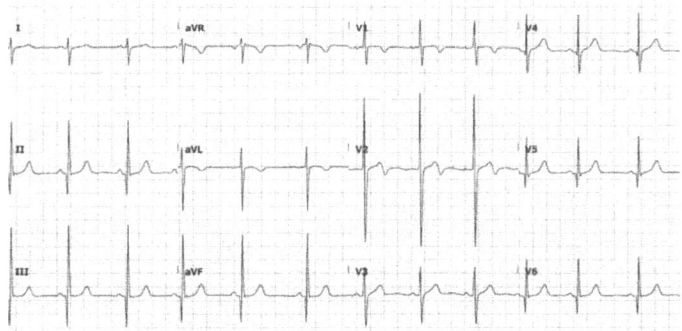

Restrictive Cardiomyopathy

Restrictive cardiomyopathy is the least common form of cardiomyopathy. It occurs in the advanced stages of myocardial infiltrative disease.

- Diffuse myocardial infiltration leafs to low voltage QRS complexes.
- Atrial fibrillation may occur due to atrial enlargement
- Infiltration of cardiac conducting system may lead to conduction disturbance.
- Healing granulomas in sarcoidosis may produces "pseudo-infraction" Q-waves.

Symptoms :-
1) Shortness of breath(at first with exercise, but eventually at rest, too)
2) Fatigue
3) Inability to exercise
4) Swelling of the legs and feet
5) Weight gain
6) Nausea, bloating and poor appetite
7) Palpitations (fluttering in the chest due to abnormal heart rhythms)

8) Fainting
9) Chest pain or pressure

Causes:-
1) Buildup of scar tissue
2) Buildup of proteins in the heart muscle (Your doctor may call this amyloidosis)
3) Chemotherapy or chest exposure to radiation
4) Too much iron in the heart `(also called haemochromatosis)
5) Other disease

ECG features :-
1) Low voltage QRS-complex
2) Non-specific ST-segment/ 'T'-wave changes
3) Bundle branch block
4) Third degree block
5) Pathological 'Q'-wave
6) Atrial and ventricular dysrhythmias.

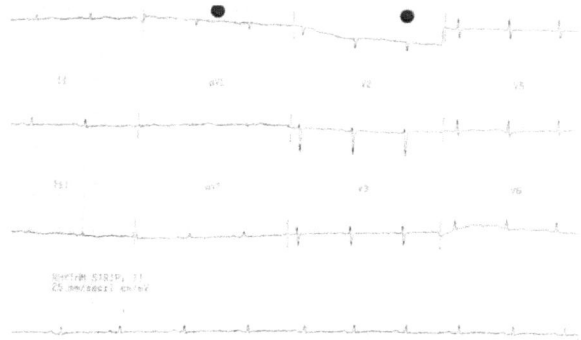

ECG of a patient with restrictive cardiomyopathy, demonstrating:

- Low voltage QRS complexes
- Widespread flattening of T waves

ECG In (VSD) Ventricular Septal Defect

Definition:- VSD is a common congenital defect most often present at birth.

It involves the hole in a wall between heart "Lower-chamber"

Symptoms: -

VSD symptoms in a baby may include

1) Poor eating
2) Fast breathing
3) Easy tiring
4) Slow growth rate
5) Shortness of breath
6) A build up of blood and fluid in the lungs
7) Weakness or fatigue, especially among infacts while eating.
8) Pale skin coloration.
9) Frequent respiratory infections.
10) Bluish skin colour, especially around lips, and nails.

Causes:-
1) Genetic and environmental factors may paly a role
2) Improper development of heart during pregnancy.

Types :-
1) Conal septal VSD
2) Peri-membranous VSD
3) Atrio-ventricular canal VSD
4) Muscular VSD

OR
1) Small [less than or equal to 3mm]
2) Medium [3 to 6mm]
3) Large [greater than 6mm]

ECG :-

1) Small VSD :-
1) Restrictive VSD QP/QS<1.5/1.0. QP/QS is pressure gradient between pulmonary and systemic circulation. ECG is normal
2) Few patients will have rsR' inv1

2) Medium VSD :-
1) Left atrial overload_ broad notched 'P'-wave.
2) Left ventricular overload_deep "Q"-wave, Tall "R"-wave, Tall "T"-wave in lead v5-v6 .
3) Atrial fibrillation can be seen.

3) Large VSD :-

1) In adults or adolescence with a large VSD and pulmonary vascular obstructive disease. LVH is absent because volume overload of the LV is no longer.
2) Large VSD will produce RVH and RAD. At this point there is either an rsR' pattern in right pre-cordial lead or more commonly, a Tall "R"-wave in right pre-cordial leads.
3) Deep "S"-wave in lateral pre-cordial leads and Tall peaked "P"-wave .
4) In patients with an acquired infundibular stenosis the ECG shows a pattern of RVH.

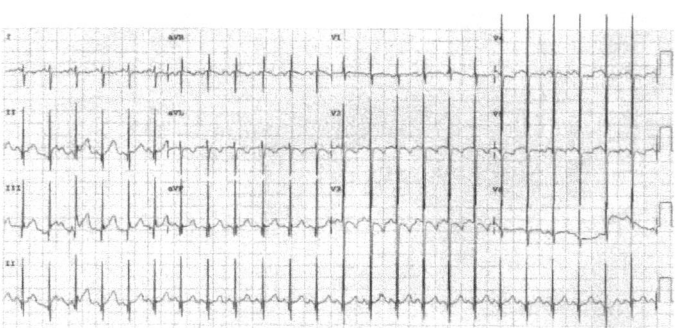

VSD with large left to right shunt

ECG In Atrial Septal Defect (ASD)

Definition :- An atrial septal defect is a hole in the wall between two upper chamber of heart.

Symptoms :-
1) Shortness of breath
2) Fatigue
3) Swelling of ankles, legs.
4) Heart palpitations.
5) Stroke

Causes:- Improper development of fetal heart during pregnancy.

Types :-
1) Ostium secundum
2) Ostium primum
3) Sinus venosus
4) Coronary sinus.

ECG in ostium secundum ASD :-

This is the most common type of ASD and occurs in middle of the wall between atria.

ECG features :-

1) Complete RBBB or incomplete RBBB
2) Right axis deviation
3) Prolongation of PR interval (first degree) AV block
4) Notched 'R'-wave in inferior limb leads.
5) If the defect is very large, severe atrial dilatation results in atrial flutter
6) In adults patients with ASD, closure of the defect does not decrease the incidence of atrial fibrillation.

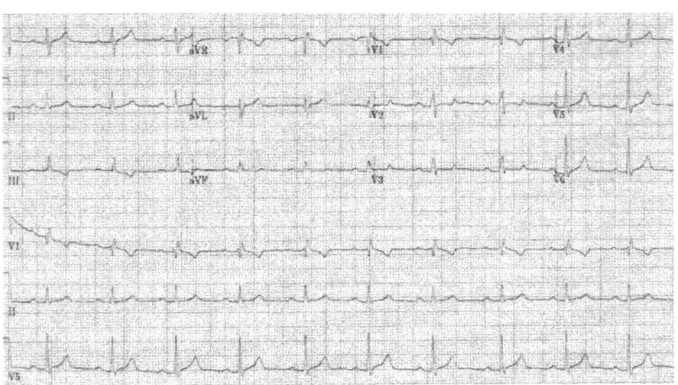

ECG in ostium primum :-

ECG in ostium primum

1) rsR' pattern in v1
2) Left axis deviation due to absence of left anterior fascicle
3) Complete or incomplete RBBB

Rhythms

4) Prolongation of PR- interval = first degree AV block.

ECG

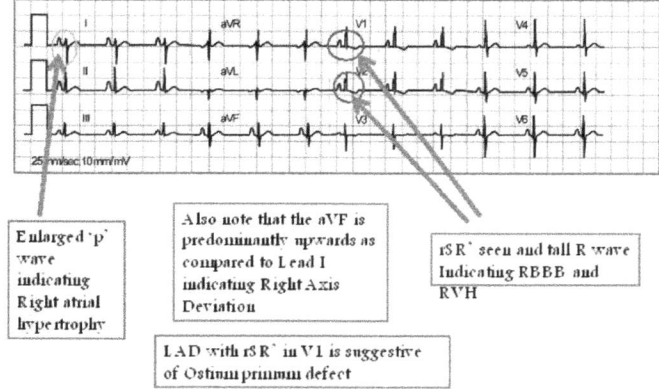

Enlarged 'p' wave indicating Right atrial hypertrophy

Also note that the aVF is predominantly upwards as compared to Lead I indicating Right Axis Deviation

rSR' seen and tall R wave Indicating RBBB and RVH

LAD with rSR' in V1 is suggestive of Ostium primum defect

ECG in sinus venosus ASD

1) Right axis deviation
2) Ectopic atrial rhythm may seen
3) Negative 'P'-waves in II, III, avF.
4) Frequent atrial pre-mature contractions.
5) Supra-ventricular tachycardia.
6) Varying degree of AV blocks
7) Sick sinus syndrome seen after closure of sinus venosus types of ASD.

ECG In (PDA) "Patent Ductus Arteriosus"

Definition: - PDA is a persistent connection between the aorta and pulmonary artery resulting in L-R shunting

Causes:-
1) Genetic factors
2) Idiopathic

Symptoms :-
1) Sweating while crying
2) Poor eating
3) Rapid heart rate

Risk factor :-
1) Pre-term birth
2) Congenital rubella syndrome
3) Genetic conditions.

ECG features in PDA :-
1) Left atrial abnormality
2) Left ventricular hypertrophy

3) If PDA is large or if there is aortic-pulmonary window, then pulmonary hypertension may develop and result in bi-ventricular hypertrophy pattern.
4) Prolongation of PR interval
5) Deep "S"-wave in v1.
6) Tall "R"-wave in v5-v6.

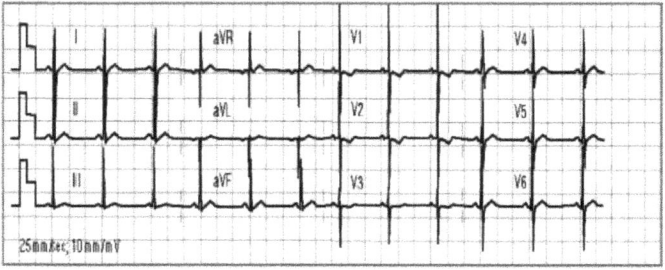

ECG In TOF

Tetralogy of fallot

TOF is a cardiac anomaly that refers to a combination of four related heart defects that commonly occur together.

1) Ventricular septal defect
2) Pulmonary stenosis
3) Over-riding aorta
4) Right ventricular hypertrophy.

Symptoms :-

1) Bluish coloration of skin [due to low O2]
2) Shortness of breath
3) Loss of consciousness
4) Poor weight gain
5) Prolonged crying

Causes:- TOF occurs during fetal growth when a baby's heart is developing while factors such as poor maternal nutrition, viral illness or genetic disorders increase the risk of this conditions.

ECG features in TOF: -

1) In the new born the ECG may be normal but over the first weeks of the life normal regression of right ventricular pre-ponderance is not seen.
2) "RVH" is the hallmark of ECG finding in patient with TOF and is of value in the differential diagnosis from VSD.
3) Tall "R"-waves in right pre-cordial lead [v1-v2]
4) Right axis deviation may accompany right ventricular hypertrophy, additionally right atrial enlargement is manifested by Tall "P"-waves.
5) Left axis deviation suggests an associated complete AV-canal.
6) Sudden transition of QRS-complex morphology in v1 and v2 is common pattern in patients with TOF.
7) There is RS pattern with a tall 'R'-wave in v1 'rs' pattern from v2 or v3 to v6.

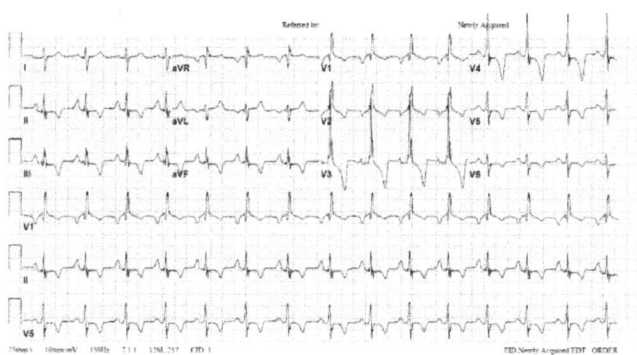

ECG In Rheumatic's

What is rheumatic heart disease?

Rheumatic heart disease is a condition in which the heart valves have been permanently damaged by rheumatic fever.

The heart valve damage may start shortly after untreated or under-treated strepto-coccal infection such as strep throat or scarlet fever.

Symptoms:- Rheumatic fever signs and symptoms which result from inflammation in the heart, joints, skin or central nervous can include.

1) Fever
2) Painful and tender joints most often in the knees, ankles, elbows and wrist.
3) Pain in one joint that migrates to another joint.
4) Red, hot or swollen joints.
5) Small, painless bumps beneath the skin
6) Chest pain.

Causes:-
- Rheumatic fever can occur after a throat infection from a bacteria called group "A" streptococcus. Group "A" streptococcus infections of the throat cause strep throat.
- Group "A" streptococcus infections of the skin or other parts of the body rarely triggers rheumatic fever.
- The link between the strep infection and rheumatic fever isn't clear, but it appears that the bacteria trick the immune system.
- The strep bacteria contain a protein similar to one found in certain tissues of the body. The body's immune system, which normally target's infection causing bacteria, attacks its own tissue, particularly tissues of the heart, joints, skin and central nervous system

Risk factor :-
1) Family history
2) Type of strep bacteria
3) Environment factors.

Types of rheumatic heart disease :-
1) Valvular heart disease
2) Peri-carditis.
3) Endo-carditis
4) Heart blocks

Valvular heart disease:- In the heart valve disease one or more valves in your heart doesn't work properly. Your heart has four valves that keep blood flowing in the correct direction. In some cases, one or more of the valve doesn't open or close properly. This can cause the blood flow through your heart to your body to be disrupted.

Symptoms:-
1) Abnormal sound [heart murmur]
2) Chest pain
3) Abnormal swelling
4) Fatigue
5) Shortness of breath
6) Dizziness
7) Fainting
8) Irregular heart beats.

Causes:-
1) Regurgitation
2) Stenosis
3) Atresia.

Risk factor:-
1) Older age
2) History of certain infections that can affect the heart.
3) Heart attack
4) High blood pressure
5) High cholesterol

6) Diabetes
7) Congenital heart disease.

- **Regurgitation**

What is regurgitation?

Regurgitation is the name for leaking heart valve. Further they are divided into

1) Mitral regurgitation
2) Aortic regurgitation
3) Pulmonary regurgitation
4) Tricuspid regurgitation

Mitral regurgitation -

ECG in mitral regurgitation :-

What is regurgitation?

It is the condition in which the heart's mitral valve "doesn't close tightly" which allows blood to flow backward in heart.

Causes :-

1) Mitral valve prolapse
2) Damaged heart tissue cords.
3) Rheumatic fever
4) Prior heart attacks
5) High blood pressure
6) Congenital heart disease
7) Endocarditis
8) Cardiomyopathy.

Symptoms :-
1) Abnormal heart sound
2) Dyspnea
3) Palpitations
4) Breathlessness
5) Swollen feets.

ECG In Mitral Regurgitation
1) **Left atrial enlargement :-**
   - Broad, bifid 'P'-wave in lead II [p-mitrale]
   - Enlargement of the terminal negative portion of the 'P'-wave in v1.
   - 'P'-wave amplitude >2.5mm in inferior leads [II, III, avF] Or >1.5mm in v1/v2 ['P'-pulmonale]

2) **Left ventricular enlargement:-** Left ventricular enlargement is associated with an increased QRS voltage on ECG and a strain pattern or inverted check mark pattern to the 'T'-wave in the lateral leads.

3) **Atrial fibrillation:-** AF is commonly seen with mitral regurgitation this is identified as an irregularly irregular rhythm with absence of "P"-waves.

4) **Pulmonary hypertension:-**
   1) Right axis deviation
   2) R/S ratio >1 in v1
   3) 'R'-wave >7mm in v1
   4) rsR1 complex in v1 with R1>10mm
   5) qR complex in v1

Rhythms

6) Right ventricular strain pattern: ST segment and 'T'-wave inversion in v1-v3 and in inferior leads [II, III, avF]
7) Right bundle branch bock:- QRS deviation >0.12 sec rsR1 in leads v1 and v2 wide slurred 'S'-wave in lateral leads [v5,v6,I]

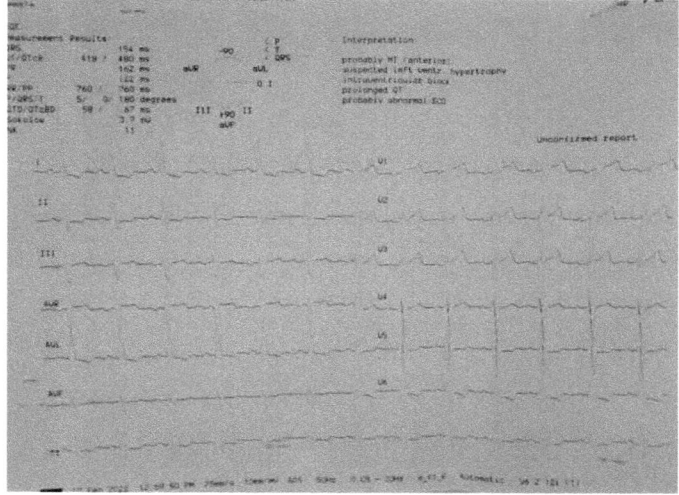

ECG In Mitral Stenosis

1) **Left atrial enlargement :-**
   - Left atrial enlargement produces a broad, bifid 'P'-wave in lead II [P-mitrale] and enlarges the terminal negative portion of the 'P'-wave in v1

2) **Right ventricular hypertrophy:-**
   - Right axis deviation of +90 Degrees
   - Rv1=7mm or more.
   - Rv1+Sv5 or Sv6=10mm or more.
   - R/S ratio in v1=1.0 or more.
   - S/R ratio in v6=1.0 or more.
   - Late intrinsicoid deflection in v1[0.35+]
   - Incomplete RBBB pattern
   - ST-T strain pattern in 2, 3, avF
   - P-pulmonale
   - s1 s2 s3 pattern in children
   - Tall 'R'-wave in v1
   - 'R'-wave greater than 'S'-wave in v1
   - 'R'-wave progression reversal

- Inverted 'T'-wave in the anterior precordial leads.

3) **Right axis deviation:-** In right axis deviation the mean QRS axis in the frontal plane moves toward the right as pulmonary hypertension worsens.

4) **Atrial fibrillation:-** Atrial fibrillation is commonly seen with mitral stenosis. AF is characterized by an irregularly irregular rhythm with absent 'P'-waves.

ECG IN MITRAL STENOSIS:-

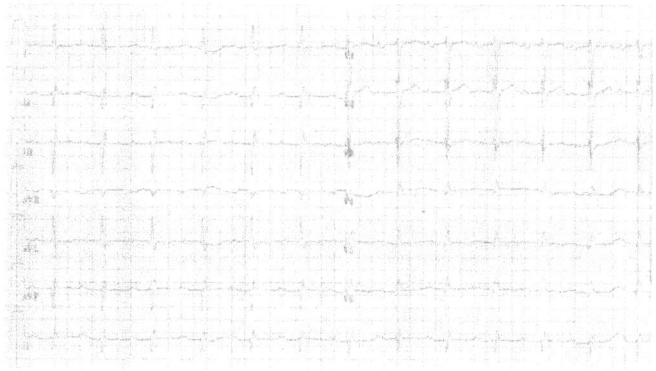

ECG In Aortic Regurgitation

What is aortic regurgitation ?

It is the condition that occurs when your heart aortic valve doesn't close tightly. Aortic regurgitation allows some of the blood that was pumped out of your heart's main pumping chamber.

Causes :-

    3) Congenital heart Valve disease

    4) Age related changes to the heart

    5) Endocarditis

    6) Rheumatic fever

    7) Trauma

Symptoms :-

    1) Shortness of breath with exercise

    2) Fatigue and weakness

    3) Fainting

    4) Irregular pulse

    5) Heart murmur

ECG in A. R:-

    1) Tachycardia

    2) Left ventricular Hypertrophy:-

Criteria for diagnosing LVH

- There are numerous criteria for diagnosing LVH, some of which are summarised below.
- The most commonly used are the SOKOLOV-LYON criteria ['S'-wave depth in v1+ tallest 'R'-wave height in v5-v6>35mm]
- Voltage criteria must be accompanied by non-voltage criteria to be considered diagnostic of LVH.
- Limb leads :-
  1) 'R'-wave in lead I+ 'S'-wave in lead III>25mm
  1) 'R'-wave in avL >11mm
  2) 'R'-wave in avL >20mm
  3) 'S'-wave in avR >14mm
- Pre-cordial leads :-
  1) 'R'-wave in v4, v5 or v6>26mm
  2) 'R'-wave in v5 or v6 plus 'S'-wave in v1>35mm
  3) Largest 'R'-wave plus largest 'S'-wave in precordial leads >45mm

3) **Left Atrial Enlargement:-** LAE produces a broad ,bifid 'P'-wave in lead II [P-mitrale] and enlarges the terminal negative portion of the 'P'-wave in v1 .

➤ In lead II :-
  - Bifid 'P'-wave with>40ms between two peaks.
  - Total 'P'-wave duration >110ms.

- In lead v1 :-
  - Bi-phasic 'P'-wave with terminal negative portion >40ms deviation
  - Bi-phasic 'P'-wave with terminal negative portion >1mm deep.

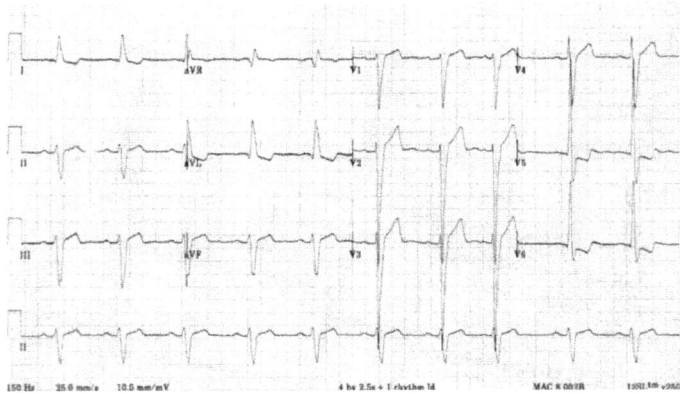

ECG In Aortic Stenosis

What is aortic stenosis?

Aortic valve stenosis occurs when the heart's aortic valve narrows. This narrowing parents the valve from opening fully, which reduces or blocks blood flow from your heart into the main artery toyour body and onward to the rest of your body.

Symptoms :-

1) Abnormal heart sound
2) Chest pain
3) Dizzy
4) Fatigue
5) Heart palpitations
6) Not eating enough
7) Not gaining enough weight

Causes :-

1) Congenital heart defect
2) Calcium build up on the valve
3) Rheumatic fever
4) History of infections that can affect heart
5) Chronic kidney disease

ECG In Aortic Stenosis
1) Left ventricular hypertrophy :-

- There are numerous criteria for diagnosing LVH some of which are summarised below.
- Most commonly used are the SOKOLOV-LYON criteria
- Voltage criteria :-
- Limb leads :-

1) 'R'-wave in lead I+ 'S'-wave in lead III >25mm
2) 'R'-wave in avL >11mm
3) 'R'-wave in avF >20mm
4) 'S'-wave in avR >14mm

- Precordial leads :-

1) 'R'-wave in v4, v5 or v6>26mm
2) 'R'-wave in v5 or v6 plus 'S'-wave in v1>35mm
3) Largest 'R'-wave plus largest 'S'-wave in precordial leads >45mm.

2) Left Atrial Enlargement:-

In lead I :-

- Bifid 'P'-wave with >40m/s between two peaks
- Total 'P'-wave duration>110ms.

In lead v1 :-

- Bi-phasic 'P'-wave with terminal negative portion>40ms duration.

- Bi-phasic 'P'-wave with terminal negative portion>1mm

3) ST-segment depressed in avL, v5 and v6.
4) 'T'-wave inversion avL, v5, v6
5) ST-segment depression exceeding 0.3mv in A.S indicates the LV strain and LVH.

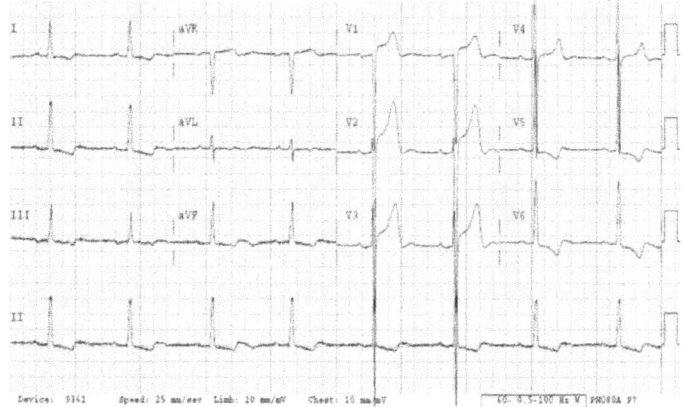

ECG In Tricuspid Stenosis

Defination: Narrowig of the tricuspid orifice that obstructs the blood flow from right atrium to right ventricle.

Causes:
1) Rheumatic heart disease.
2) Congenital malformations.
3) Infective endocarditis.

Symptoms:
1) fatigue
2) enlarged liver
3) cold skin
4) shortness of breath

ECG in tricuspid stenosis:
1) Tall "P" waves in lead II III and avF
2) Right ventricular hypertrophy
3) right atrial enlargement

Rhythms

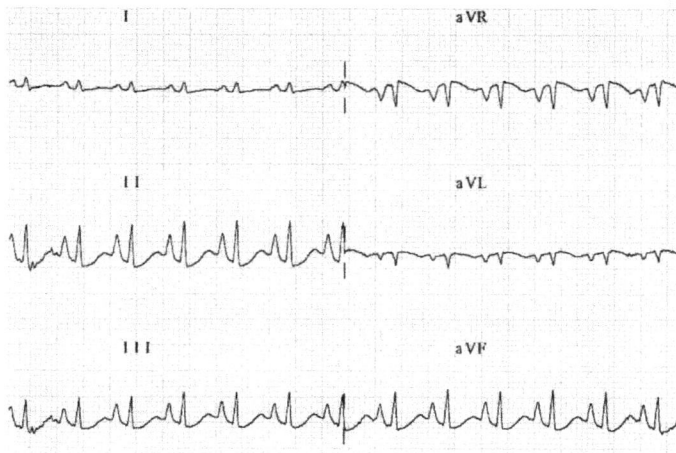

- Right atrial enlargement: P pulmonale
- P wave amplitude > 2.5mm in leads II, III and aVF

ECG In Tricuspid Regurgitation

Defination:

It happens when the triscupid vakve in the heart doesn't seal shut entirely. This allows the blood to flow backwards and the more backwards blood flow the more severe it is.

Causes:

1) Ebsteins anomaly
2) Infective endocarditis
3) Carcinois syndrome
4) Endomyocardial biopsy
5) Rheumatic fever

Symptoms:

1) fatigue
2) declining exercise capacity
3) abnormal heart rhythms
4) pulsing in your necl
5) shortness of breath with activity

ECG in tricuspid regurgitation:
1) p pulmonale
2) right axis deviation
3) right ventricular hypertrophy
4) tall R waves in V1 and v2
5) inverted T waves in anterior precordial leads
6) R waves greater than S wave in V 1

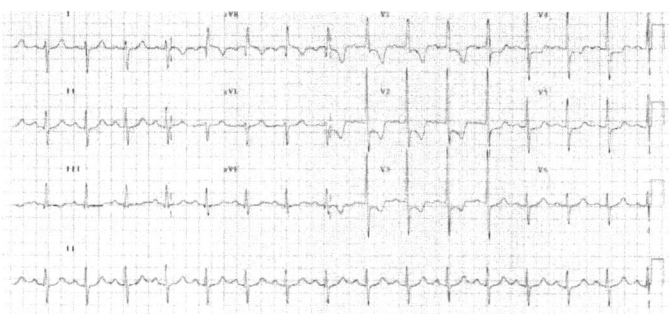

ECG In Pulmonary Stenosis

Pulmonary stenosis: when the pulmonary valve between RV and pulmonary atery is too small narrow. pulmonary valve opening slows the blood

Causes:

Pulmonary valve stenosis occurs when the pulmonary valve doesn't grow properly during the fetal growth babies who have the condition may have the other congenital heart abnormalities as well. It is not known what causes the valve to develop abnormally.

Symptoms :
1) heart murmur
2) fatigue
3) shortness of breath
4) chest pain
5) loss of consciousness

ECG:
1) 1 ECG may be found Normal in some patients with mild pulmonary stenosis.
2) Right axis deviation: sometimes this may be the only ecg abnormally in mild pulmonary stenosis,

severe pulmonary stenosis will result in significant right axis deviation.

3) In Moderate pulmonary stenosis: "R" wave amplitude in leas V1 increases in RSR' pattern may be observed in lead V1.
4) If pulmonary stenosis is severe the R wave amplitude in V1 may be >20mm
5) RVH
6) In patients with severe pulmonary stenosis Q wave may be seen in V1 to V3.

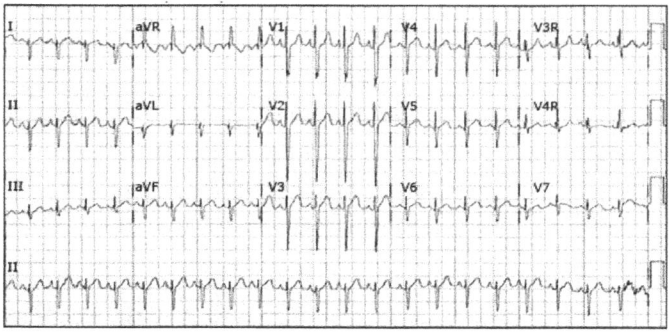

ECG In Pulmonary Regurgitation

Pulmonary regurgitation is a condition which occurs when the pulmonary valve doesn't completely close and allows some blood leak back into the heart

Symptoms:
1) chest pain
2) difficulty in breathing
3) fainting
4) swelling of legs and feet
5) irregular heart beats

Cause:
1) infective endocarditis
2) TOF
3) pulmonary hypertension
4) congenital heart disease

ECG In Pulmonary Regurgitation:

Commonly seen ecg in pulmonary regurgitation is the absence of pulmonary artery hypertension are rsR. configuration in the right pre-cordial leads which reflects RV diastolic overload. If it is secondary to PAH, then p-pulmonale (Tall p waves indicating right atrial enlargement) increased r to s ratio in right precordial leads along with RAD can be seen.

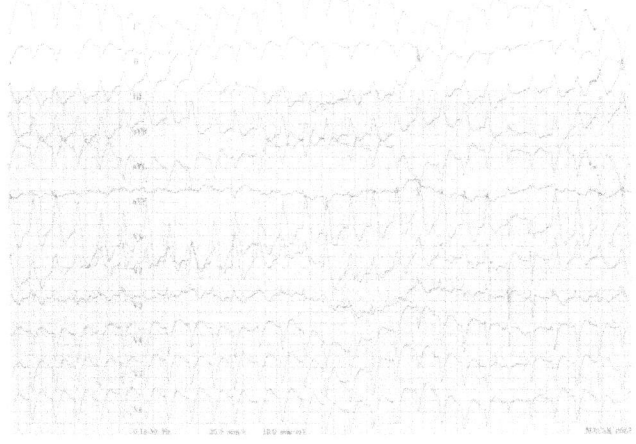

ECG In Dextrocardia

Definition:- Dextro-cardia occurs when the heart is positioned in the right side of the chest instead of the left.

Causes:-

1) Genetic causes
2) During the early pregnancy [6th week] the baby's heart develops the reasons for the dextrocardia are unclear.

Symptoms:-

1) Bluish skin
2) Difficulty breathing
3) Failure to grow and gain weight
4) Fatigue
5) Jaundice (yellow skin and eyes)
6) Pale skin(pallor)
7) Repeated sinus or lung disease

ECG:-

1) Right axis deviation
2) Positive 'QRS' complexes [with upright 'P' and 'T'-waves in avR]
3) Lead I: Inversion of all complexes, aka "global negatively" [Inverted 'P'-wave, negative QRS, inverted 'T'-wave]
4) Absent 'R'-wave progression in the chest leads [Dominant 'S'-waves through out]

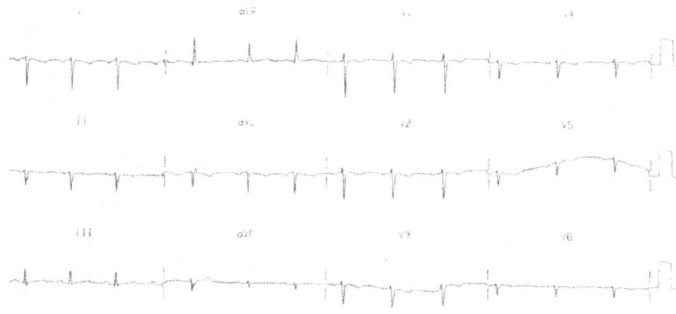

Ebstein Anomaly

Ebstein Anomaly is rare heart defect that's present at birth. In this condition your tricuspid valve is in the wrong position and the valve's flaps are in the incorrect shape.

Symptoms:-
1) Shortness of breath
2) Fatigue
3) Arrhythmias
4) Cyanosis

Causes:-
1) Defect may be present at birth
2) Holes in the heart
3) Arrhythmias
4) Wolff Parkinson white [wpw] syndrome.

ECG In Ebstein's Anomaly
- The ECG is abnormal in most patients with Ebstein's Anomaly.
- It may show tall and broad 'P'-waves as result of right atrial enlargement.

Rhythms

- Prolonged PR-interval
- Complete or incomplete right bundle branch block.
- The 'R'-waves in lead v1 and v2 are small.
- Bizarre morphologies of the terminal QRS pattern result from conduction disturbances and abnormal activation of the atrialized right ventricle.
- Atrial flutter
- Atrial fibrillation

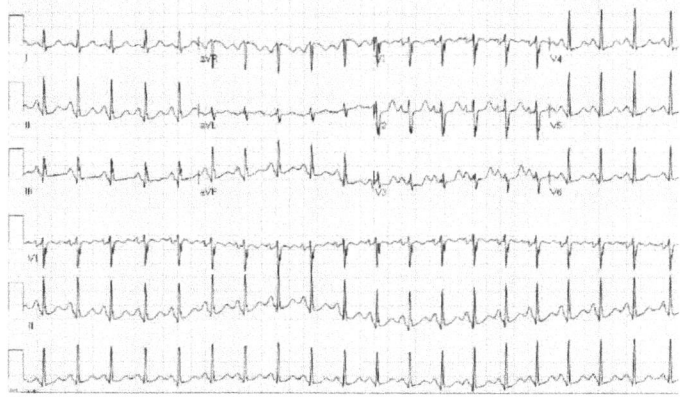

Coarctation Of The Aorta

Coarctation of the aorta is the congenital condition characterised by narrowing of the aorta near the site where the ductus arteriosus insertus.

Causes :-
1) Condition is generally present at birth.
2) Traumatic injury.
3) Severe hardening of the arteries.
4) Inflamed Arteries.

Symptoms :-
1) Pale skin
2) Heavy swelling
3) Difficulty breathing
4) Difficulty feeding
5) High blood pressure
6) Headaches
7) Muscle weakness
8) Leg cramps
9) Nose blood
10) Chest pain.

ECG :-

In infants and adolescent's an aortic coarctation may be asymptomatic on an ECG and show no evidence of abnormal tracings. This is generally true for milder forms of aortic coarctation. Patients with additional associated congenital heart disease may have abnormal ECG tracing as a result of the complications interactions of multiple conditions, In infants severe aortic coarctation will present in right ventricular hypertrophy.

In order adolescents and adults, milder forms of the coarctation may present with a normal ECG more severe coarctations will present in left ventricular hypertrophy. Where there are 'T'-waves and ST-segment changes found in the left pre-cordial leads.

Infective Endocarditis

Infective endocarditis is a disease characterized by inflammation of the endocardium typically affecting the heart valves and usually caused by infection and can be acute, sub acute or chronic.

Causes :-

- Organisms:-
    1) Staphylococcus aureus
    2) Coagulase negative staphylococcus
    3) Streptococcus viridans
    4) Streptococcus bovis
    5) Enterococcus [coccus]
- Culture Negative Endocarditis: -
    1) Brucella
    2) Bartonella
    3) Coxiella burnetti
    4) Chlamydia
    5) Legionella.

Symptoms:-

1) Flu-like symptoms, such as fever and chills
2) A new or changed heart murmur, which is the heart sounds made by blood rushing through your heart
3) Fatigue
4) Aching joints and muscles
5) Night sweats
6) Shortness of breath
7) Chest pain when you breathe
8) Swelling in your feet, legs or abdomen

ECG:-

1) 'p'-mitrale
2) Widening PR interval
3) Dysrhythmia
4) 'T'-wave inversion.

Truncus Arteriosus

Truncus Arteriosus is a heart defect that is a present at birth. It happens when there is an abnormal connection between the aorta and pulmonary artery. Normally, the aorta and pulmonary artery are separate.

Causes:-

1) Genetic

Symptoms:-

1) Bluish colour to the skin
2) Problems breathing
3) Poor feeding
4) Tiredness
5) Enlarged liver.

ECG:-

ECG findings in young infants with truncus arteriosus do not distinguish this lesion from others on the differential diagnosis.

A normal sinus rhythm, normal intervals, and either a normal QRS axis or minimal right Axis deviation are generally observed. Biventricular hypertrophy is a characteristic finding.

In patient with substantial pulmonary over circulation left ventricular forces are especially prominent with evidence of left atrial enlargement

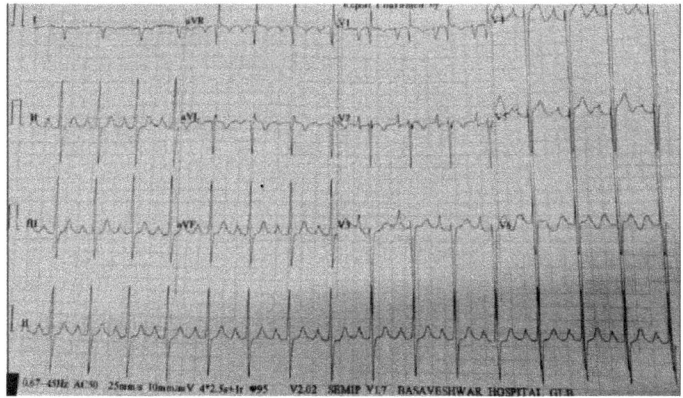

Tricuspid Atresia

Tricuspid atresia is a heart defect present at birth in which a tricuspid valve between two of the heart's chamber isn't formed.

Instead there's solid tissue between the chamber's which restricts blood flow and causes the right lower heart chamber (ventricle) to be underdeveloped.

Symptoms :-
1) Blue tinge to the skin
2) Difficulty breathing
3) Tiring easily
4) Slow growth and poor weight gain
5) Fatigue and weakness.

Causes :-

Tricuspid atresia occurs during fetal heart development. Some genetic factors such as down syndrome, might your body risk of congenital heart defects such as tricuspid atresia.

ECG :-

1) Common ECG pattern of tricuspid atresia is left axis deviation, tall, peaked and occasionally notched 'P'-waves.

2) Left ventricular pre-dominance in pre-cordial leads were found in the majority of cases.

3) The PR interval is usually normal but either abnormal prolongation or shortening may be present.

4) The lack of consistent ECG evidence of left ventricular hypertrophy is contrasted with the anatomic left ventricular hypertrophy which is invariably present.

5) Majority of cases in which there is normal axis and all cases in which there is right axis deviation are associated with either pulmonic atresia or transposition of the great vessels with large pulmonary artery.

Rhythms

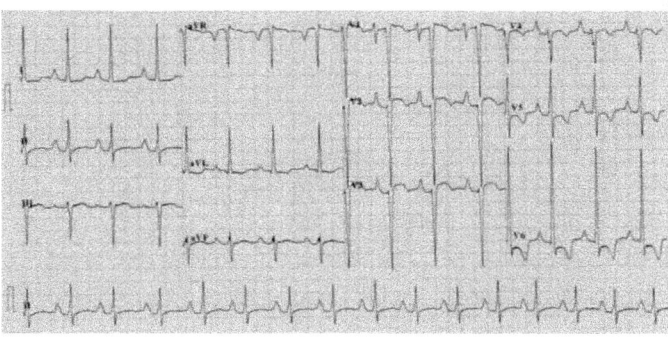

ECG Features In Atrial Fibrillations

1) Irregularly irregular rhythm
2) No 'P'-waves
3) Absence of an iso-electric baseline
4) Variable ventricular rate
5) Fibrillation waves may be present and can be either fine (amplitude <0.5mm) or cause (amplitude >0.5mm)
6) Fibrillatory waves may mimic 'P'-waves leading to misdiagnosis
7) QRS complexes usually <120ms unless pre-existing bundle branch block, accessory pathway or rate related aberrant conduction.

Other features:-
1) The ventricular response and thus ventricular rate is AF is dependent on several factors including vagal tone, other pace maker foci, AV node function, refractory period and medication
2) Commonly AF is associated with a ventricular rate ~110-160.

Classification of Atrial Fibrillation:-

- First episode – Initial defection of AF regardless of symptoms
- Re-current AF – More than 2 episode of AF
- Paroxysmal AF – Self terminating episode < 7 days.
- Persistent AF – Not self-terminating, duration > 7days.
- Long standing persistent AF - > 1year.
- Permanent AF - Duration > 1year in which rhythm control interventions are not pursued.

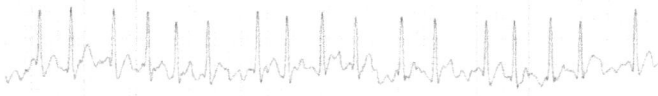

Atrial Flutter

Atrial flutter is a type of supra-ventricular tachycardia caused by re-entry circuit within the right atrium. The length of the re-entry circuit corresponds to the size of the right atrium, resulting in a fairly pre-dictable atrial rate around 300bpm.

Causes:-

1) Ischaemia: Lower blood flow to the heart due to coronary heart disease, hardening of the arterites, or a blood clot

2) Hypertension: high blood pressure

3) Cardiomyopathy: Disease of the heart muscle

4) Abnormal heart valves: Especially the mitral valve

5) Hypretrophy: An enlarged chamber of the heart

6) Open-heart surgery

Symptoms:-

1) Palpitations (rapid heartbeat or a pounding or fluttering sensation in the chest)

2) Shortness of breath

3) Anxiety

4) Angina pectoris (chest or heart pain)
5) Syncope (fainting)

ECG :-
General features :-
- Narrow complex tachycardia
- Regular atrial activity at ~300bpm
- Flutter waves ("saw –tooth" pattern) best seen in leads II, III, avF may be more upside down.
- Flutter waves in v1 may resemble 'P'-waves
- Loss of the iso-electric baseline.
- **Fixed AV Blocks**

Ventricular rate is a fraction of the atrial rate example:-
- 2:1 block =150bpm
- 3:1 block =100bpm
- 4:1 block =75bpm.
- **Variable AV blocks**
  - Ventricular response is irregular and may mimic Atrial Flutter.
  - On closer inspection there may be a pattern of alternating 2:1, 3:1 and 4:1 conduction ratios.

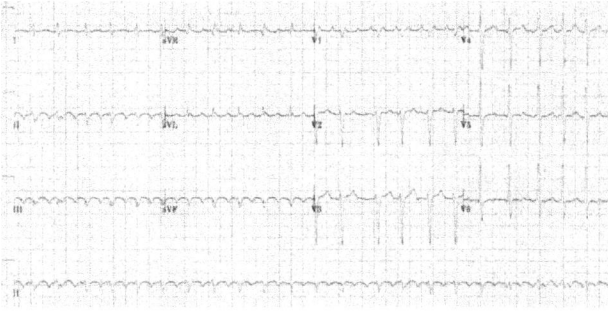

Pre-Mature Atrial Complex

Atrial ectopic and pre-mature atrial complex [PAC]. These arise from ectopic pacemaking tissue within the atria. There is abnormal 'P'-waves, usually followed by a normal QRS complex.

Causes:-

1) Pregnancy
2) High blood pressure, heart disease, or hyperthyroidism
3) Stress or fatigue
4) Caffeine
5) Alcohol

Symptoms: -

1) A flutter in your chest
2) Fatigue after exercise
3) Shortness of breath or chest pain
4) Light headedness or dizziness

ECG:-

1) An abnormal (non-sinus) 'P'-wave is followed by a QRS complex
2) The 'P'-wave typically has a different morphology and axis to the sinus 'P'-waves.

3) Abnormal 'P'-wave may be hidden in the preceding 'T'-wave producing a "peaked" or "camel hump" appearance if this is not appreciated the PAC may be mistaken for a PTC.

4) PAC's arising close to the AV-node activate the atria retrogradely, producing an inverted 'P'-wave with a relatively short PR-interval ≥120ms.

5) PAC's that reach the SA node may depolarise it causing the SA node to "reset" this result in a longer than normal interval before the next sinus beat arrives.

6) PAC's arriving early in the cycle may be conducted aberrantly usually with a RBBB morphology. They can be differentiated fromPAC's by the presence of a preceding 'P'-waves.

7) Similarly, PAC's arriving very early in the cycle may not be conducted to the ventricles at all. In this case, you will see an abnormal 'P'-wave that is not followed by a QRS complex. It is usually followed by a compensatory pause as the sinus node resets.

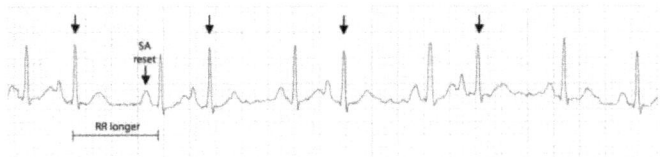

Benign Early Reproduction

'BER' is an ECG pattern most commonly seen in young, healthy patients < 50 years of age.

ECG :-
1) Widespread concave ST elevation, most prominent in the mid to left pre-cordial leads [v2-v5]
2) Nothing or slurring at the 'J'-point
3) Prominent slightly assymetrical 'T'-waves that are con-cordant with QRS complex.
4) The degree of ST elevation is modest in comparison to the 'T'-wave amplitude.
5) ST elevation is usually <2mm in the pre-cordial leads and <0.5mm in the limb leads, although pre-cordial STE may be up to 5mm in some instances.
6) No reciprocal ST depression to suggest STEMI
7) ST changes are relatively stable over time.

ST segment / 'T'-wave Morphology.

The ST segment – 'T'-wave complex in BER has a characteristic appearance

- There is elevation of the 'J'-point.

- The 'T'-wave is peaked and slightly asymmetrical.
- The ST segment and the ascending limb of the 'T'-wave form an upward concavity
- The descending limb of the 'T'-wave is straighter and slightly steeps than the ascending limb.
- The concept of "smiley-shaped" ST elevation [popularized by Ken Grauer in 1993] is worthy of mention.

"Smiley –shaped" ST elevation is GREAT visualaid but you may want to describe upward concavity or ST coving to your consulting Cardiologist"

J point morphology

One characteristic feature of BER is the presence of a notched or irregular 'J'-point the so called "fish hook" pattern. This is often best seen in lead v4.

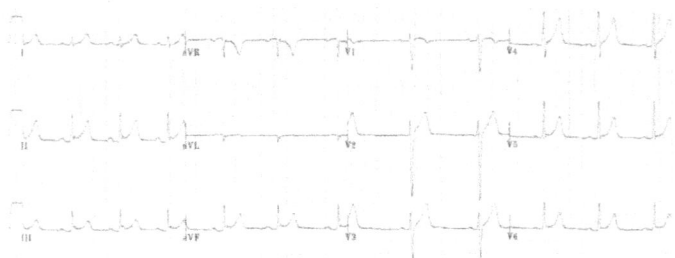

Beta Blocks Toxicity

Effects on the ECG :-
1) Sinus bradycardia
2) 1st degree, 2nd degree, 3rd degree AV block
3) Junctional bradycardia
4) Ventricular bradycardia

A prolonged PR-interval is an early sign of beta blocks even in the absence of significant bradycardia.

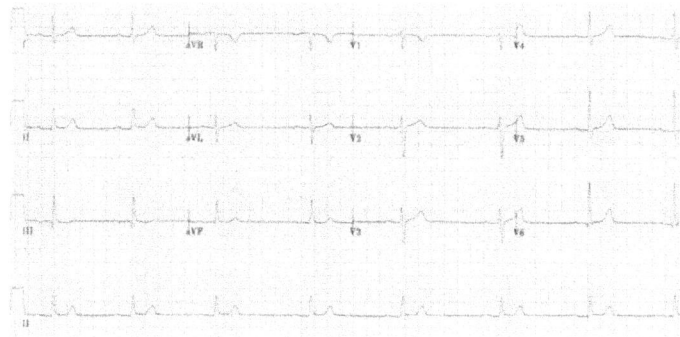

Bi-Directional Ventricular Tachycardia (BVT)

BVT is a rare ventricular dysrhythmia characterised by a beat to beat alternation of the frontal QRS axis.

Causes :-
- This rhythm is most commonly associated with severe digoxin toxicity
- BVT is also been reported with herbal aconite poisoning

Symptoms :-
- Chest pain
- Dizziness
- Shortness of breath
- Feeling as if your heart is racing (palpitations)
- Lightheadedness

Rhythms

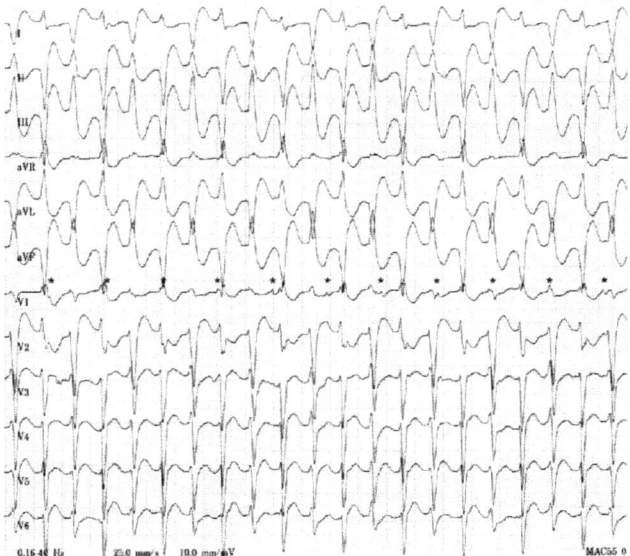

Brugada Syndrome

Brugada syndrome is an ECG abnormality with a high incidence of sudden death in patients with structurally normal hearts.

Diagnostic Criteria

Type I :-
1) Covered ST segment elevation >2mm in 1 or v1 to v2 followed by negative 'T'-wave.
2) This is the only ECG abnormality that is potentially diagnostic.
3) It is often referred to as brugada sign.

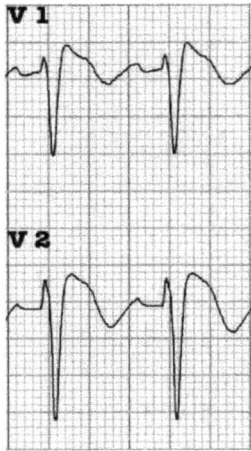

Rhythms

Type II :-
1) Brugada type 2 has > 2mm of saddle shaped ST elevation.

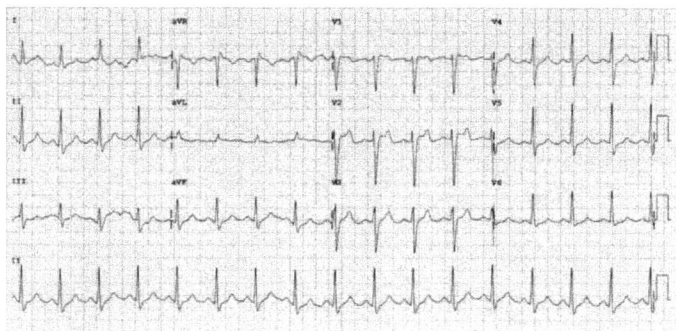

Type III :-
1) Brugada type 3 :- can be the morphology of either type I or II , but with <2mm of ST segment elevation.

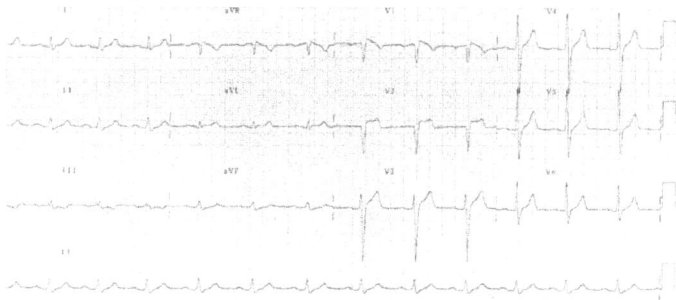

Calcium Channel Blocks Toxicity

Effects on the ECG :-

1) Sinus bradycardia
2) 1st degree , 2nd degree , 3rd degree , AV block
3) Junctional bradycardia
4) Ventricular bradycardia

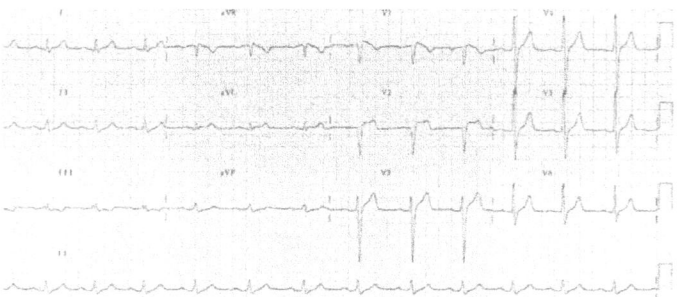

Carbamazepine Cardiotoxicity

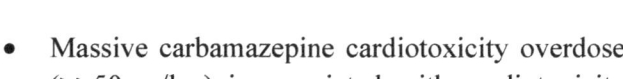

- Massive carbamazepine cardiotoxicity overdose (>>50mg/leg) is associated with cardiotoxicity due to fast sodium channel blockade.

- This may be detectable on the ECG as subtle QRS widening or 1st degree AV block.

- ECG changes are not usually as dramatic as those seen in the context of TCA overdose.

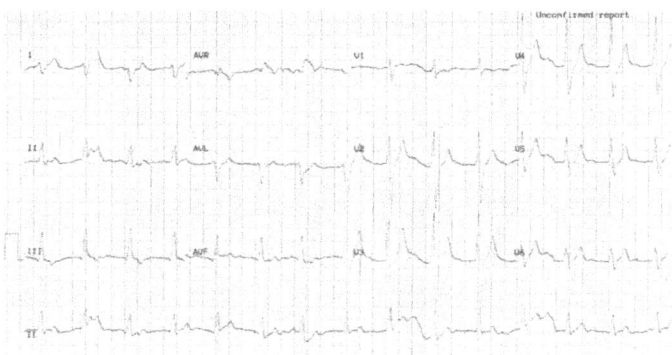

ECG In COPD Chronic Obstructive Pulmonary Disease

COPD:- Chronic Obstructive pulmonary disease (COPD) is chronic inflammatory lung disease that causes obstructed airflow from the lungs.

Causes :-
1) Smoking
2) Expose to fumes from burning fuel
3) Poorly ventilated homes

Symptoms :-
1) Frequent respiratory infections
2) Wheezing
3) Chest tightness
4) Lack of energy
5) Unintended weight loss (in later stages)

ECG features in COPD

ECG changes occur in COPD due to

- Presence of hyper expanded emphysematous lungs with the chest

- The long term effects of hypoxic pulmonary vasoconstriction upon the right side of the heart, causing pulmonary hypertension and subsequent right atrial and right ventricular hypertrophy.

Typical ECG finding in COPD :-

1) The most typical ECG finding in emphysema are :-
   - Right shift of the 'P'-waves axis with prominent 'P'-waves in the inferior leads and flattened or inverted 'P'-waves in leads I and avL.
   - Rightward shift of the QRS axis towards +90 degrees or beyond.
   - Exaggerated atrial depolarization causing PR and ST segments that "sag" below the TP baseline.
   - Low voltage QRS complexes, especially in the left pre-cordial leads [v4-v6]
   - Clockwise rotation of the heart with delayed R/S transition point in the pre-cordial leads +/- persistent 'S'-waves in v6. There may be complete absence of 'R'-waves in leads v1-v3

2) With development of cor-pulmonale the following additional changes are:-
   1) Right atrial enlargement
   2) Right ventricular hypertrophy

3) Other ECG changes that may be seen
   1) RBBB
   2) Multifocal atrial tachycardia

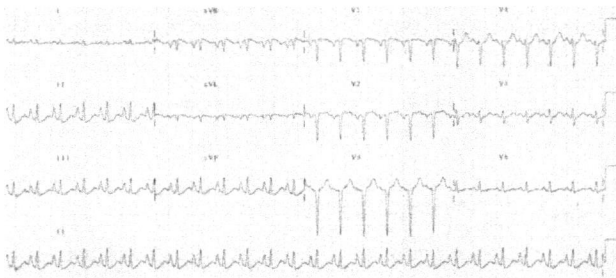

Digoxin Effect

ECG features demonstrating the digoxin effect: -

❖ Digoxin effect refers to the presence on the ECG of:-

- Downsloping ST depression with a characteristic "Salvador dali sagging" appearance.
- Flattened inverted, or biphasic 'T'-waves.
- Shortened QT interval

Other digoxin effect features
- Mild PR interval prolongation of up to 240ms
- Prominent 'U'-waves
- Peaking of the terminal portion of the 'T'-waves
- 'J'-point depression

QRS complex / ST- segment changes

The morphology of the QRS complex / ST segment is variously described as either "slurred", "sagging" or "scooped" and resembling either a "reverse trick" "honey stick" "Salvador Dali's moustache"!

'T'-waves changes :-

The most common 'T'-wave abnormality is biphasic 'T'-wave with an initial negative deflection and terminal positive deflection. This is usually seen in leads with a dominant "R"-wave. [v4-v6].

The first part of the 'T'-wave is typically continuous with the depressed ST segment. The terminal positive deflection may be peaked, or have a prominent 'U'-wave superimposed upon it.

Mechanism:- ECG features of digoxin effect are seen with therapeutic doses of digoxin and are due to :-

1) Shortening of the atrial and ventricular refractory periods producing a short QT interval with secondary repolarisation abnormalities affecting the ST segments 'T'-waves and 'U'-waves.

2) Increased vagal effects at the AV node causing a prolonged PR interval.

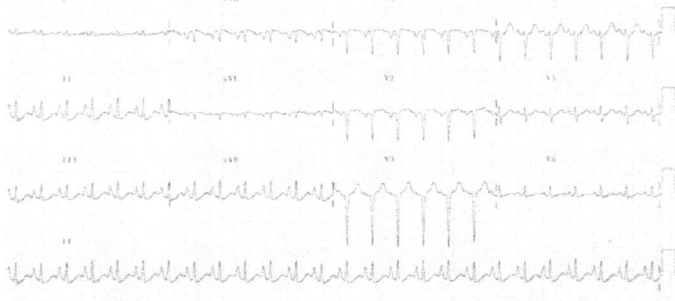

Digoxin Toxicity

ECG features of digoxin toxicity

The classic digoxin toxic dysrhythmia combines:-

- Supra ventricular tachycardia [due to increased automaticity]
- Slow ventricular response [due to decreased AV conduction]

Other common dysrhythmias associated with digoxin toxicity include:-

- Frequent pvcs [most common abnormality including ventricular bigeminy and trigeminy]
- Sinus bradycardia
- Slow atrial fibrillation
- Any type of AV block
- Ventricular tachycardia, including polymorphic and bi-directional VT.

Hypercalcaemia

Definition:- Hypercalcemia is a condition in which the calcium level in your blood is above normal.

Causes:-
1) Hyperparathyroidism
2) Myeloma
3) Bony metastases
4) Paraneoplastic syndrome
5) Milk-alkali syndrome
6) Sarcoidosis
7) Excess vitamin 'D'

Symptoms:-
1) **Kidneys:** - Excess calcium makes your kidneys work harder to filter it.

2) **Digestive system:** - Hypercalcemia can cause stomach upset, nausea, vomiting and constipation.

3) **Bones and muscles:** - In most cases, the excess calcium in your blood was leached from your bones, which weakens them.

4) **Brain:** - It causes confusion, lethargy and depression

5) **Heart:** - causes palpitations and fainting, arrhythmia.

ECG:-

1) The main ECG abnormality seen with hypercalcaemia is shortening of the QT-segment
2) In severe hypercalcaemia, Osborn waves ['J'-waves] may be seen.
3) Ventricular irritability and VF arrest has been reported with extreme hypercalcaemia.

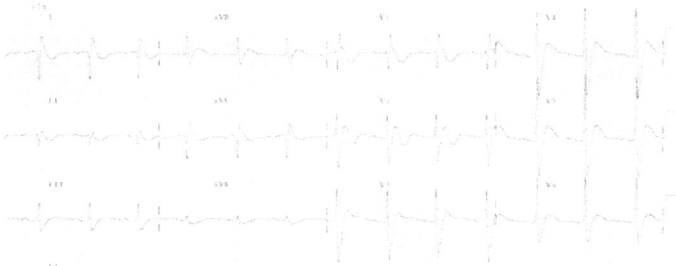

Hyperkalaemia

Definition:- It is a condition the potassium level is higher than normal in your blood .

Causes:-
1) Kidney: - Hyperkalaemia happen if your kidneys do not work. It is a job of kidneys to balance of the amount of potassium taken in with the amount lost in urine.
2) A diet high in potassium: - Eating too much food that is high in potassium can also cause hyperkalaemia.
3) Breaking down red blood cells
4) Breaking down of muscle tissue
5) Hormonal diorders

Symptoms:-
1) Muscle weakness
2) Muscle cramps
3) Nausea
4) Difficulty in breathing
5) Chest pain

Effects of hyperkalaemia on ECG:-

Serum potassium> 5.5mEq/L is associated with repolarisationabnormalities :-

- Peaked 'T'-waves [usually the earliest sign of hyperkalaemia]

Serum potassium >6.5mEq/L is associated with progressive paralysis of the atria.

- 'P'-wave widens and flattens
- PR segment lengthens
- 'P'-waves eventually disappear.

Serum potassium >7.0mEq/L is associated with conduction abnormalities and bradycardia :-

- Prolonged QRS interval with bizarre QRS morphology
- High- grade AV block with slow junctional and ventricular escape rhythm
- Any kind of conduction block[bundle branch blocks, fascicular block]
- Sinus bradycardia or slow AF
- Development of asine wave appearance [a pre-terminal rhythm]

Serum potassium level of >9.0mEq/L causes cardiac arrest due to :-

- Asystole
- Ventricular fibrillation

- PEA with bizarre, wide complex rhythm.

ECG manifestations in hyperkalaemia

- Peaked 'T'-waves
- Prolonged PR-segment
- Loss of 'P'-waves
- Bizarre QRS complexes
- Sine wave

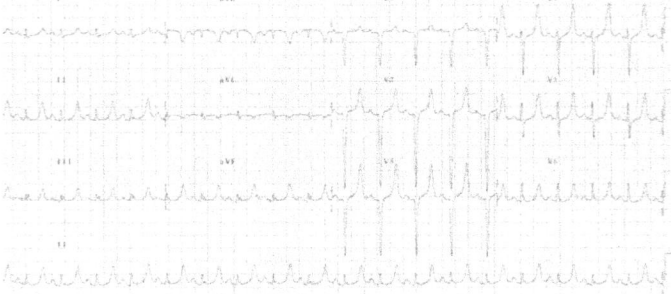

Hyperthyroidism

Definition:- Hyperthyroidism is underactive thyroid disease, is common disorder, your thyroid gland does not make enough thyroid hormones.

Symptoms:-
1) Changes in menstrual cycle
2) Dry hair and hair loss
3) Constipation
4) Dry skin
5) Puffy face

Causes :-
1) Disorder of hypothalamus
2) Pituitary gland damage
3) Problems with thyroid with birth
4) Inflammation to the thyroid gland
5) Pregnancy

ECG:- The most common ECG changes seen with thyrotoxicosis are :-
- Sinus tachycardia
- Atrial fibrillation with rapid ventricular response

- High left-ventricular voltage "voltage criteria" for LVH. Without evidence of LV strain.

Other ECG abnormalities include :-
- Supraventricular arrhythmias [premature atrial beats, paroxysmal supraventricular tachycardia]
- Multifocal atrial tachycardia, atrial flutter
- Ventricular extra systoles.
- Non-specific ST and 'T'-wave changes.

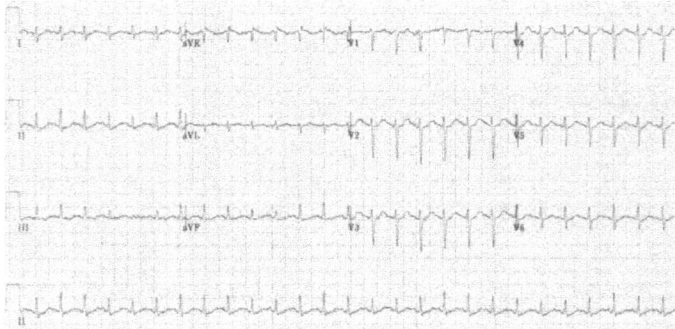

Hypercalcaemia

Definition :- It is condition in which the calcium level in your blood is above normal

Symptoms :-
1) Kidney:- Excess calcium makes your kidneys work harder to filter it. This can cause excessive thirst and frequent urination.
2) Digestive system: - Hypercalcaemia can cause stomach upset, nausea, vomiting and constipation
3) Bones and muscle:- In most cases, the excess calcium in your blood was leached from your bones, which weakens them. This can cause bone pain and muscle weakness.

Causes :-
1) Cancer:- Lungs cancer, breast cancer, blood cancer
2) Hypoparathyroidism
3) Vitamin 'D' deficiency
4) Acute pancreatitis
5) Hypomagnesaemia

ECG :-

1) Hypocalcaemia causes QTc-prologation primarily by prolongation the ST segment
2) The 'T'-wave is typically left unchanged
3) Dysrhythmia's are uncommon, although atrial fibrillation has been reported.
4) Torsades de pointes may occur, but is much less common than with hypokalaemia or hypomagnesaemia.

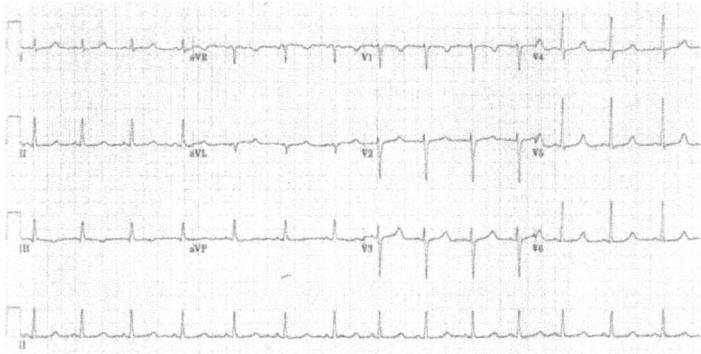

Hypokalaemia

Definition :- A blood level that is below normal in potassium an important body chemical. The problem can result in fatigue.

Causes :-
1) Vomit
2) Diarrhea
3) Drinking too much
4) Folic acid deficiency

Symptoms :-
1) Fatigue
2) Weakness
3) Constipations
4) Arrhythmia

ECG :- Changes occurs when k + <2.7mm01 /1
- Increased amplitude and width of the 'P'-wave
- Prolongation of the PR interval
- 'T'-wave flattening and inversion
- ST depression

- Prominent 'U'-waves
- Apparent long QT-interval due to fusion of the 'T'-waves and 'U'-waves.

With worsening hypokalaemia

- Frequent supraventricular and ventricular ectopics
- Supraventricular tachyarrhythmias :- AR, atrial flutter, atrial tachycardia.
- Potential to develop life threatening ventricular arrhythmias eg VT, VF and torsades de pointes.

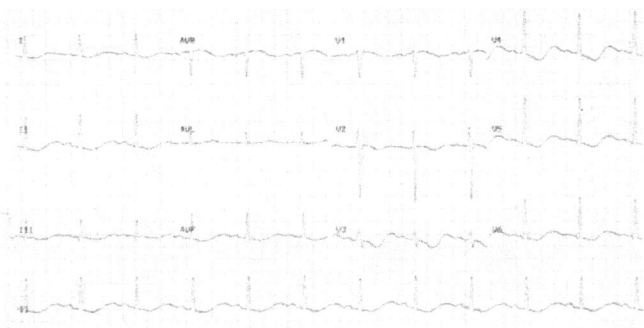

Hypomagnesaemia

Definition :- It is an electrolyte disturbance caused when there is a low level of serum magnesium in the blood [less than 1.46 mg/dL].

Causes :-

1) GI disease
2) Type 2 diabetes
3) Alcohol dependence
4) Use of diuretics

Symptoms:-

1) Nausea
2) Vomiting
3) Weakness
4) Decreased appetite

ECG :-

- Primary ECG abnormality seen with hypomagnesaemia is a prolonged QTc.
- Atrial and ventricular ectopy atrial tachyarrhythmias and torsades de pointes are seen in context of hypomagnesaemia, although

whether this is a specific effect of low serum magnesium or due to concurrent hypokalaemia is uncertain.

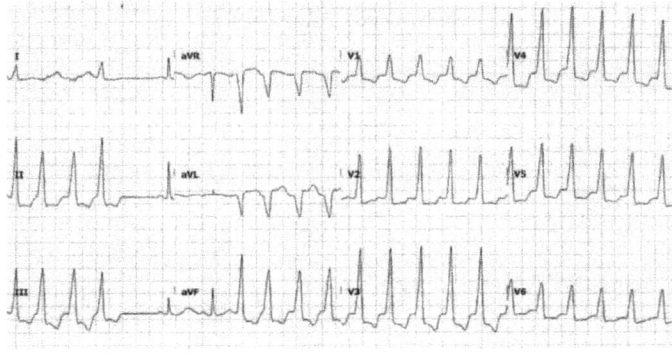

Hypothermia

Definition:- Hypothermia is defined as a core body temperature q <35 degree c.

- Mild hypothermia is 32–35-degree c.
- Moderate hypothermia is 29–32-degree c.
- Severe hypothermia is <29degree c.

Symptoms :-
1) Slow, shallow breathing
2) Confusion
3) Slurred or mumbled speech
4) A slow, weak pulse
5) Loss of co-ordination.

Causes :-
1) Cold exposure
2) Diabetes
3) Thyroid conditions
4) Alcohol

ECG :-

1) Bradyarrhythmia
2) Osborne waves
3) Prolonged PR, QR intervals
4) Shivering artefact
5) Ventricular ectopics.
6) Cardiac arrest due to VT, VF.

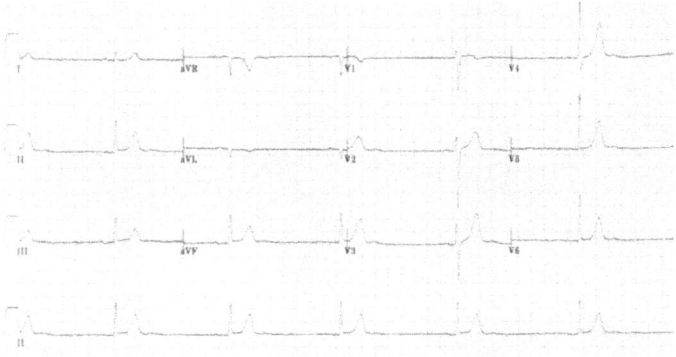

Hypothyroidism

Definition:- Abnormally low activity of the thyroid gland, resulting in retardation of growth and mental development in children and adults.

Causes:-
1) Autoimmune disease
2) Over response to hyperthyroidism treatment
3) Thyroid surgery
4) Radiation therapy
5) Medications

Symptoms :-
1) Fatigue
2) Increased sensitivity to cold
3) Dry skin
4) Thinning hair
5) Puffy eyes
6) Depression

ECG :- Severe hypothyroidism(myxoedema) causes a
- Bradycardia
- Low QRS voltage
- Widespread 'T'-wave inversions

- QT prolongation
- First AV block
- Interventicular conduction delay.

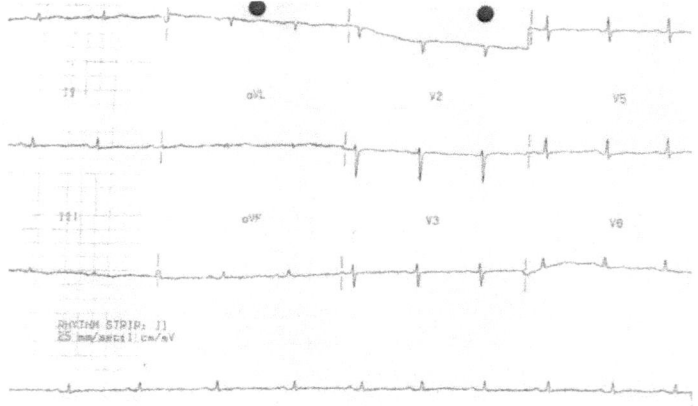

Intracranial Pressure

Definition:- It is defined as the pressure within the craniospinal compartment , a closed system that comprises a fixed volume of neutral tissue , blood and cerebrospinal fluid.

Causes :-
1) Tumor
2) Bleeding into the brain
3) Swelling within the brain

Symptoms :-
1) Subarachnoid haemorrhage
2) Intraparenchymal haemorrhage
3) Massive ischaemic stroke causing cerebral ocdema.

ECG :-
- Widespread giant 'T'-waves inversions.
- QT prolongations.
- Bradycardia.
- ST segment elevation / depressions – this may mimic myocardial ischaemia.
- Increased 'U'-waves amplitude.

- Other rhythm disturbances : sinus tachycardia.
- Junctional rhythms, premature ventricular contractions atrial fibrillations.

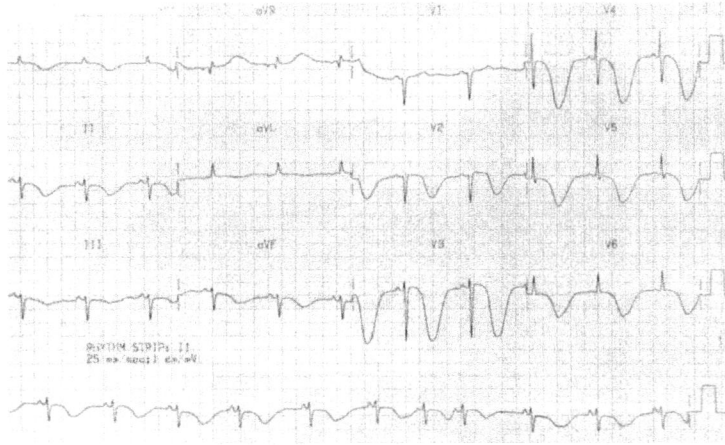

Intrinsicoid Deflection

Intrinsicoid deflection ['R'-wave peak time]. The time from the onset of the 'R'-wave in the lateral leads [avL, v5-v6].

- Represents the time taken for excitation to spread from the endocardial to the epicardial surface of the LV.
- 'R'-wave peak time is said to be prolonged if >45ms
- Additionally used in lead II in the differentiation of ventricular tachycardia (VT) and supraventricular tachycardia (SVT) with aberrancy.

Causes of prolonged RWPT
- Left anterior fascicular block
- Left ventricular hypertrophy
- Left bundle branch block

RWPT In wide QRS complex tachycardia

RWPT can be used in differentiating ventricular tachycardia from supraventricular tachycardia in patients with wide QRS complex tachycardia.

RWPT duration is measured in lead II from the onset of QRS depolarization until the first change of polarity (with both positive or negative QRS deflection).

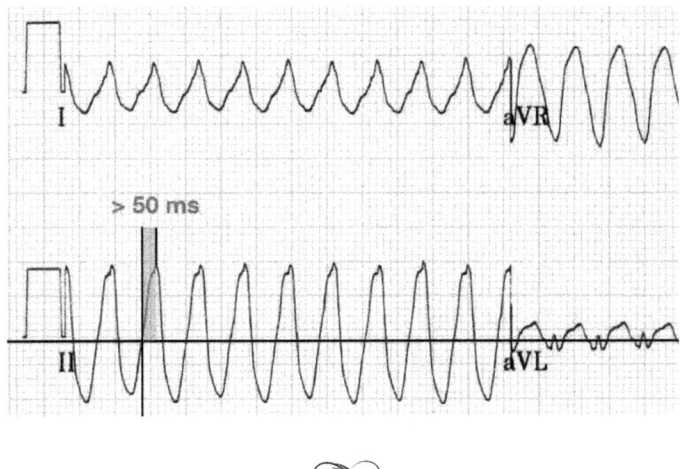

Junctional Premature Beat Or Premature Junctional Complex

A premature junctional is → A premature beat arising froman ectopic focus within the AV junction.

Origin of ectopic beats :-

- Groups of pacemaker cells throughout the conducting system are capable of spontaneous depolarisation.

- The rate of depolarisation decreases from top to bottom : fastest at the sino atrial node ; slowest within the ventricles.

- Etopic impulses from subsidiary pacemaker normally suppressed by more rapid impulses from above.

- However if an ectopic focus depolarises early enough –before the arrival of the next sinus impulse – it may "capture" the ventricle, producing a premature contraction.

- Premature contractions("etopics") are classified by their origin – atrial (PAC's) , junctional (PJC's) or ventricular (PVC's).

ECG features :-

- Narrow QRS complex, either (1) without a preceding 'P'-wave or (2) with a retrograde 'P'-wave which may appear before during or after the QRS complex it before there is a short PR interval of <120ms and the "retrograde" 'P'-waves are usually inverted in leads II, III and avF.

- Occurs sooner than would be expected for the next sinus impulse.

- Followed by a compensatory pause.

- Pjc's that arrive early in the cycle may be conducted aberrantly most commonly with a RBBB morphology.

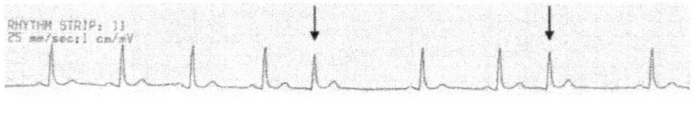

LMCA Occlusion: ST Elevation In AVR

Left main coronary artery (LMCA) overview

Typical ECG findings with LMCA occlusion :

- Widespread horizontal ST depression, most prominent in leads I, II and V4-6
- ST elevation in aVR ≥ 1mm
- ST elevation in aVR ≥ V1

ST Elevation in aVR

NOTE:- ST elevation in aVR is not entirely specific to LMCA occlusion.

ST Elevation in aVR may also be seen with:

- Proximal left anterior descending artery (LAD) occlusion. Severe triple- vessel disease (3VD).
- Diffuse subendocardial ischaemia – e.g. due to O_2 supply/demand mismatch, following resuscitation from cardiac arrest

Mechanism of ST elevation (STE) in aVR

- Lead aVR is electrically opposite to the left sided leads I, II, aVL and V4-6; therefore ST depression in these leads will produce reciprocal ST elevation in aVR.

- Lead aVR also directly records electrical activity from the right upper portion of the heart, including the right ventricular outflow tract and the basal portion of the interventricular septum. Infarction in this area could therotically produce ST elevation in aVR.

Cause of ST elevation (STE) in aVR

Two possible mechanisms:

- Diffuse subendocardial ischaemia, with ST depression in the lateral leads producing reciprocal change n aVR (=most likely).

- Infraction of the basal septum, i.e. a STEMI involving aVR.

The basal septum is supplied by the first septal perforator artery (a very proximal branch of the LAD), so ischaemia/infarction of the basal septum would imply involvement of the proximal LAD or LMCA.

Predictive value of STE in aVR

in the context of widespread ST depression + symptoms of myocardial ishaemia:

- STE in aVR ≥1mm indicates proximal LAD/LMCA occlusion or severe 3VD STE IN aVR ≥1mm predicts the need for CABG

- STE in aVR ≥V1 differentiates LMCA from proximal LAD occlusion.

- Absence of ST elevation in aVR almost entirely excludes a significant LMCA lesion In the context of anterior STEMI:

- STE in aVR ≥1mm is highly specific for LAD occlusion proximal to the first septal branch In patients undergoing exercise stress testing :

- STE of ≥1mm in aVR during exercise stress tesing predicts LMCA or ostial LAD stenosis Magnitude of ST elevation in aVR is correlated with mortality in patients with acute coronary syndromes:

- STE in aVR ≥0.5mm was associated with a 4-fold increase in mortality

- STE in aVR ≥1mm was associated with a 6- to 7- fold increase in mortality

- STE in aVR ≥1.5mm has been associated with mortalities ranging from 20 – 75%

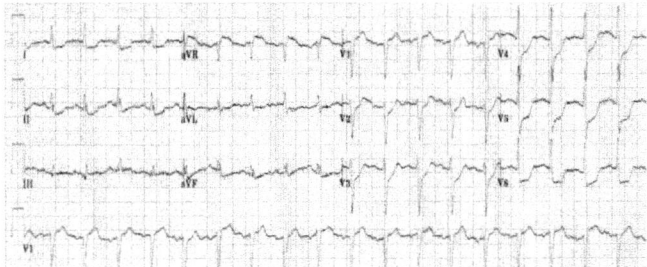

Low QRS Voltage

Low QRS Voltage Overview

The QRS is said to be low voltage when:

- The amplitude of all the QRS complexes in limb leads are < 5mm; or
- The amplitude of all the QRS complexes in the precordial leads are <10mm

Mechanisms

Low voltage is produced by....

- The "damping effect of increased layers of fluid, fat or between the heart and the recording electrode.
- Loss of viable myocardium.
- Diffuse infiltration or myxoedematous involvement of the heart.

Causes :-

The most important cause is massive pericardial effusion, which produces a triad of:

1) Low voltage
2) Tachycardia
3) Electrical alternans

Patients with his triad need to be immediately assessed for clinical or echocardiographic evidence of temponade.

Other causes of low voltage include:
- Fluid :- Pericardial effusion; Pleural effusion
- Fat :- Obesity
- Air :- Emphysema; Pneumothorax
- Infiltrative/Connective Tissue Disorders
- Myxoedema
- Infiltrative myocardial diseases – i.e. restrictive cardiomyopathy due to amyloidosis, sarcoidosis, haemochromatosis
- Constructive pericarditis
- Scleroderma
- Loss of viable myocardium: Previous massive MI; End – stage dilated cardiomyopathy

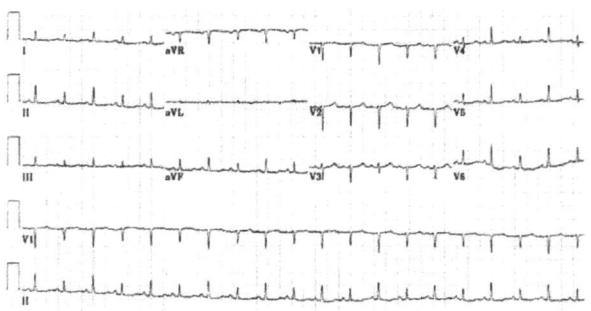

ECG Motion Artefacts

ECG Motion Artefacts Overview
- Motion artefact due to tremor or shivering can obscure the waveforms of the ECG or simulate pathology, making ECG interpretation difficult.
- In certain circumstances (e.g. hypothermia), the presence of shivering artefact may actually aid diagnosis.

Causes of Tremor:-
1) Benign Essential Tremor (physiological tremor)
2) Parkinson's Disease (intention tremor)
3) Alcohol/Benzodiazepine withdrawal
4) Anxiety
5) Thyrotoxicosis
6) Multiple sclerosis
7) Drugs: Amphetamines, cocaine, lithium.

Other types of motion artefact
1) Fever (rigors)
2) Hypothermia (shivering)
3) Cardiopulmonary resuscitation (chest compressions)

4) A non – complaint, mobile, talkative patient (=the most comon cause)!

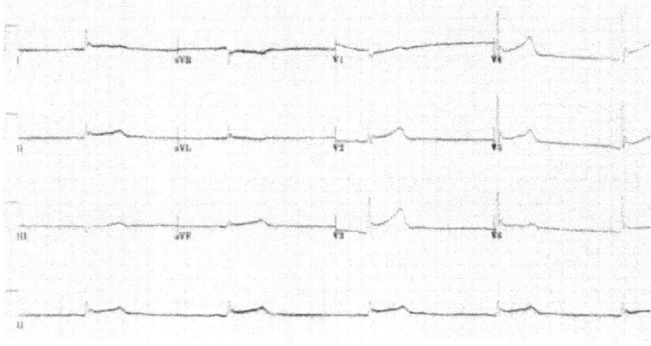

Multifocal Atrial Tachycardia (MAT)

Multifocal Atrial Tachycardia (MAT) Overview :-

- A rapid, irregular atrial rhythm arising from multiple ectopic foci within the atria.
- Most commonly seen in patients with severe COPD or congestive heart failure.
- It is typically a transitional rhythm between frequent premature atrial complexes (PACs) and atrial flutter/fibrillation.

AKA "Chaotic atrial tachycardia"

Electrocardiographic features

- Heart rate>100bpm (usually 100-150bpm; may be as high as 250bpm).
- Irregularly irregular rhythm with varying PP, PR and RR intervals.
- At least 3 distinct 'P'-wave morphologies in the same lead.
- Isoelectic baseline between 'P'-waves (i.e. no flutter waves).

- Absence of a single dominant atrial pacemaker (i.e. not just sinus rhythm with frequent PACs).
- Some 'P'-waves may be non-conducted; others may be aberrantly conducted to the ventricles.

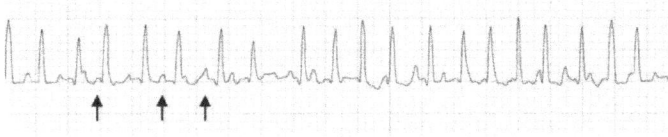

Myocarditis

Myocarditis Overview

- Myocarditis inflammation in the absence of ischaemia.
- Often associated with pericarditis, termed myopericarditis.
- Usually, a benign disease without serious long – term complications.
- In the acute setting can cause arrhythmias, cardiac failure, cardiogenic shock and death.
- May result in delayed dilated cardiomyopathy.

Causes of Myocarditis

1) Viral – including coxsackie B virus, HIV, influenza, A, HSV, adenovirus.
2) Bacteria – including mycoplasma, rickettsia, leptospira.
3) Immune mediated – including sarcoidosis, scleroderma, SLE, Kawasaki's disease.
4) Drugs/toxins – including clozapine, amphetamines.

ECG in Myocarditis

ECG changes can be variable and include :

- Sinus tachycardia.
- QRS/QT prolongation.
- Diffuse 'T'-wave inversion.
- Ventricular arrhythmias.
- AV conduction defects.
- With inflammation of the adjacent pericardium, ECG features of pericarditis can also been seen (=myopericarditis).

NB. The most common abnormality seen in myocarditis is sinus tachycardia with non-specific ST segment and 'T'-wave changes.

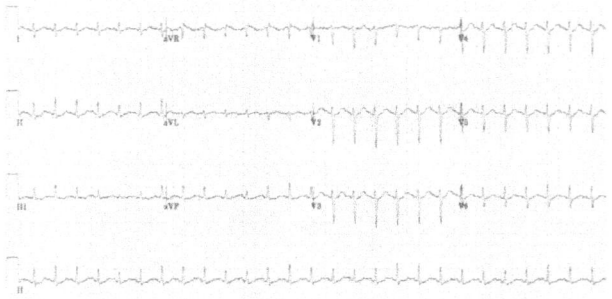

Pacemaker Rhythms – Normal Patterns

Pacemaker Components :-
1) Pulse generator
   - Power source
   - Battery
   - Control circuitry
   - Transmitter/Receiver
   - Reed switch (Magnet activated switch)
2) Lead(s)
   - Single or multiple
   - Unipolar or bipolar

Pacemaker Classification :-
- Pacemaker are classified by the nature of their pacing mode.
- Classification follows pacemaker code developed by the North American Society of pacing and Electrophysiology (NASPE) and the British Pacing and Electrophysiology Group (BPEG).

- The NAPSE/BPEG Generic (NBG) Pacemaker Code was last revised in 2002, although many textbooks still use the previous version from 1987.
- The code is expressed as a series of up to five letters.

NBG Pacemaker Code (2002)
Position I :- Chambers Paced
- Refers to chambers paced.

Position II :- Chambers Sensed
- Refers to the location where the pacemaker senses native cardiac electrical activity.

Position III :- Response to Sensing
- Refers to pacemakers response to sensed native cardiac activity.
- T = Sensed activity results in triggering of paced activity
- I = Sensed activity results in inhibition of pacing activity

Position IV :- Rate Modulation
- Indicates ability for rate modulation designed to altered heart appropriately to meet physiological needs e.g. physical activity. Sensors may measure and respond to variables including vibration, respiration, or acid- base status.

Position V :- Multisite pacing

- Allows indication of multiple stimulation sites within one anatomical area e.g. more than one pacing site within the atria or biatrial pacing.

Common Pacing Modes
AAI – Atrial pacing and sensing

- If native atrial activity sensed then pacing is inhibited.
- If no native activity sensed for pre-determined time then atrial pacing initiated.
- Used in sinus node dysfunction with intact AV conduction.
- Also termed atrial demand mode.

VVI – Ventricle pacing and sensing

- Similar to AAI mode but involving ventricles instead of the atrium.
- Used in patients with chronic atrial impairment e.g. atrial fibrillation or flutter.

DDD – Pacing and sensing the atria and ventricles

- Commonest pacing mode.
- Atrial pacing occurs if no native atrial activity for set time.
- Ventricular pacing occurs if no native ventricle activity for set time following atrial activity.

- Atrial channel function is suspend during a fixed periods following atrial and ventricular activity to prevent sensing ventricular activity or retrograde p waves as native atrial activity.

Magnet mode :-

- Applying a magnet to a pacemaker will initiate the magnet mode.
- This mode varies with pacemaker set – up and manufacturer.
- Usually initiates an asynchronous pacing mode – AOO, VOO, or DOO.
- Asynchronous modes deliver constant rate paced stimuli regardless of native rate of rhythm.
- In asynchronous ventricle pacing there is a risk of pacemaker – induced ventricular tachycardia.
- Note this differs from magnet application to an implantable cardioversion defibrillator (ICD) which results in defibrillator deactivation.

Criteria for pacemaker insertion :-

- The 2002 American college of cardiology, American Heart Association and North American Society for pacing and Electrophysiology guidelines for implantation of cardiac pacemakers.
- ACC/AHA/HRS 2008 Guidelines for Rhythm Abnormalities

Paced ECG – Electrocardiographic Features

The appearance of the ECG in a paced patient is dependent on the pacing mode used, placement of pacing leads, device pacing native electrical activity. Features of the paced ECG are: Pacing spikes

- Vertical spikes of short duration, usually 2ms.
- May be difficult to see in allleads.
- Amplitude depends on position and type of lead.
- Bipolar leads result in a much smaller pacing spike than unipolar leads.
- Epicardially placed leads result in smaller pacing spikes than endocardially placed leads.

Atrial Pacing :-

- Pacing spike precedes the p wave.
- Morphology of p wave dependent of lead placement but many appear normal.

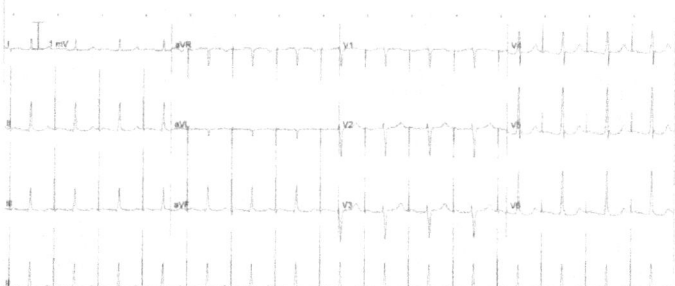

Ventricular Pacing :-
- Pacing spike precedes the QRS complex.
- Right ventricular pacing lead placement results in a QRS morphology similar to LBBB.
- Left epicardial pacing lead placement results in QRS morphology similar to RBBB.
- ST segments and T waves should be discordant with the QRS complex i.e. the major terminal portion of the QRS complex is located in the opposite side of the baseline from the ST segment and T wave.

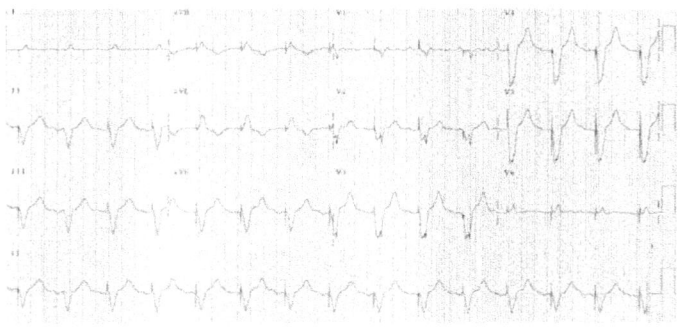

Dual Chamber Pacing:-
- Dependant on areas begin paced.
- May exhibit features of atrial pacing, ventricular pacing or both.
- Pacing spikes may precedes only P wave, only QRS complex, or both.

- The absence of paced complexes does not always mean pacemaker failure as it may reflect satisfactory native conduction. ECG Features

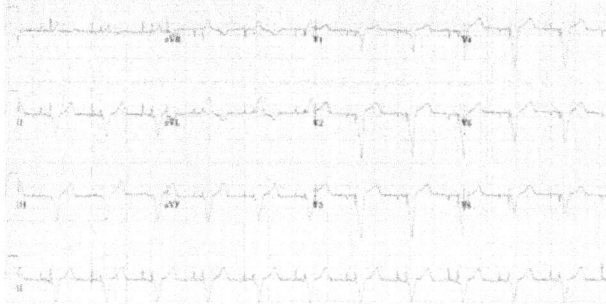

Accelerated Junctional Rhythm

Accelerated junctional rhythm [AJR] occur when the rate of AV junctional pacemaker exceeds that of the sinus node. This situation arises when there is increased automaticity in the AV node coupled with decreased automaticity in the sinus node.

Causes of AJR:-
1) Digoxin Toxicity
2) Myocardial ischaemia
3) Myocarditis
4) Cardiac surgery.

ECG:-
1) Narrow complex rhythm; QRS duration < 120ms.
2) Ventricular rate usually 60 – 100bpm.
3) Retrograde 'P'-wave may be present and can appear before, during or after the QRS complex.
4) Retrograde 'P'-wave are usually inverted in the inferior leads [I, II, aVF] upright in aVR + V1

5) AV dissociation may be present with the ventricular rate usually greater than the atrial rate.

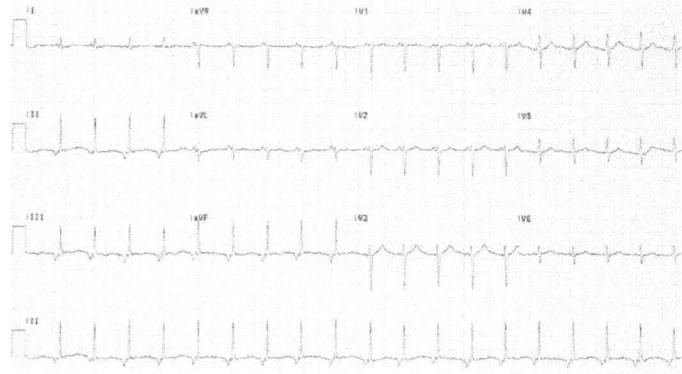

ECG Limb Lead Reversal

Overview :-

Accidental misplacement of the limb lead electrodes is a common cause of ECG abnormality and may simulate pathology such as ectopic atrial rhythm, chamber enlargement or myocardial ischaemia and infarction.

When the limb electrodes [LA, RA, LL] are exchanged without disturbing the neutral electrode (RL/N), Einthoven's triangle is "Flipped" – 180degree or rotated, resulting in leads that switch positions, become inverted or remain unchanged.

Exchanging one of the limb electrodes with the neutral electrode (RL/N) disrupts Einthoven's triangle and distorts the zero signal received from wilson's central terminal altering the appearance of both limb and precordial leads.

Limb leads may be grossly affected taking on the appearance of other leads or being reduced to a flat line.

Electrodes:-

- LA = left Arm
- RA = right Arm
- LL = left leg
- RL/N = right leg(neutral electrode)

Leads :-
- Bipolar leads I, II, III
- Augmented unipolar leads: avL, avF, aVR
- Wilson's central terminus (WCT): The "zero" lead, produced by averaging signals from the limb electrodes.

LA/RA – Reversal

With reversal of the LA and RA electrodes, Einthoven triangle flips 180 degree horizontal around an axis formed by leads avF.

This has the following effects on the ECG
- Lead I become inverted
- Lead II and III switch places
- Lead avL and aVR switch places
- Lead avF remains unchanged.

Quick guide to spotting LA/RA reversal:-
- Lead I is completely interval [P-wave, QRS complex and T-wave]
- Lead aVR often become positive.
- There may be marked right axis deviation.

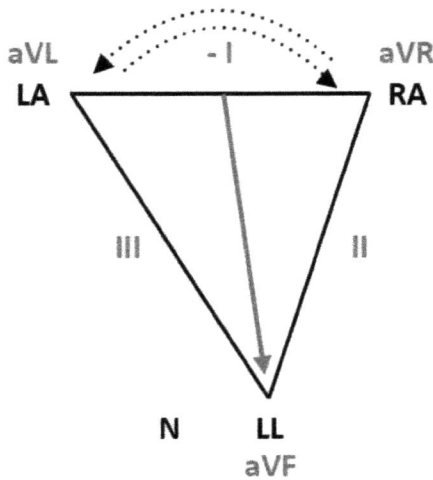

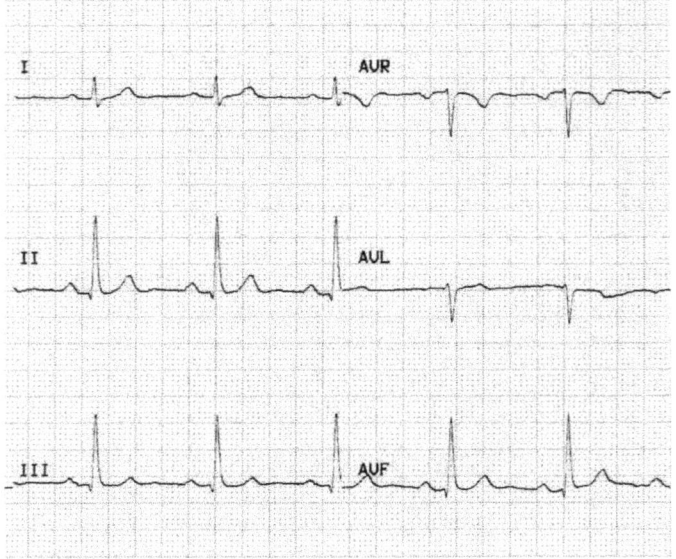

Dig. 1)Base line

2) LA/RA – Reversal

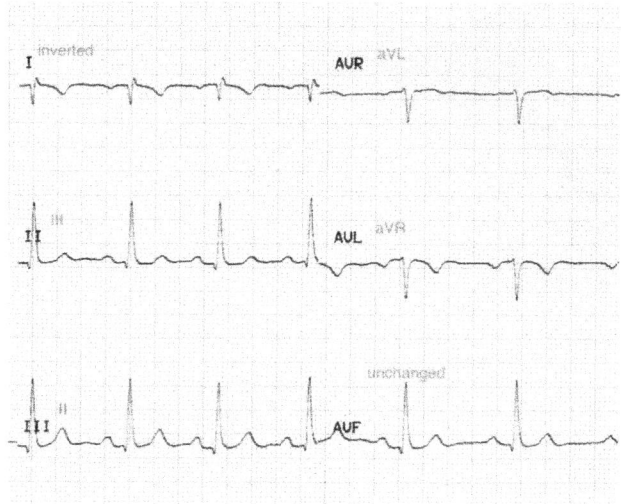

LA/LL Reversal

With reversal of the LA and LL electrodes, Einthoven's triangle rotates 180 degree vertically around an Axis formed by aVR.

This has following effects on ECG :-

- Lead III becomes inverted
- Lead I and II switch places
- Leads avL and avF switch places
- Lead aVR remains nchanged.

Quick guide to spotting LA/LL reversal :-

- Lead III is completely inverted (P-wave, QRS complex and T-wave)
- P-wave is unexpectedly larges in lead I than lead II.

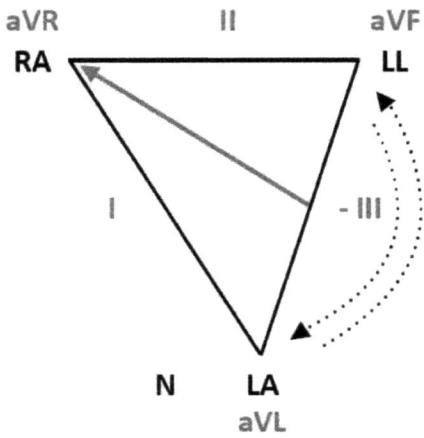
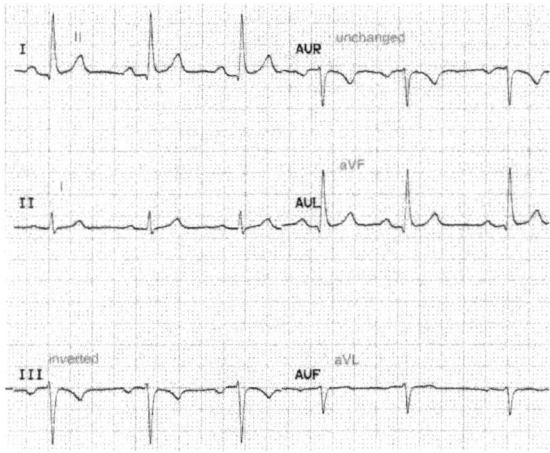

Dig. 1) LA/LL Reversal

Dig. 2) Baseline ECG

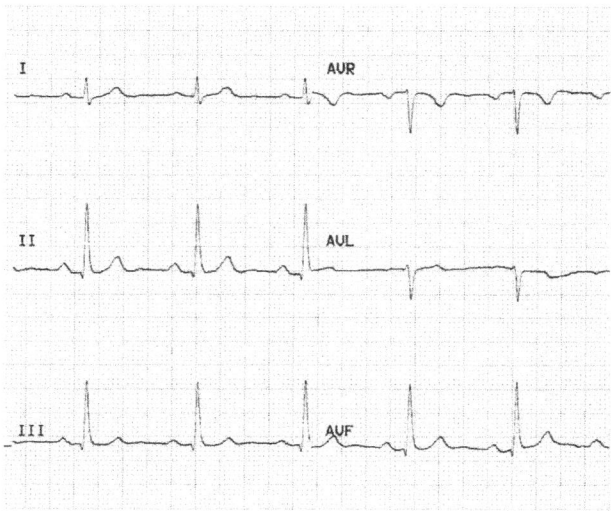

RA/LL reversal

With reversal of the RA and LL electrodes, Einthoven triangle rotates 180 degrees vertically around an Axis formed by avL.

This has thefollowing effects on the ECG :-

- Lead II becomes inverted
- Lead I and II become inverted and switch places.
- Lead aVR and avF switch places.
- Lead avL is unchanged.

Quick guide to spotting RA/LL reversal

- Leads I, II, III and avF all completely inverted [P-wave, QRS complex and T-wave]
- Lead aVR is upright.

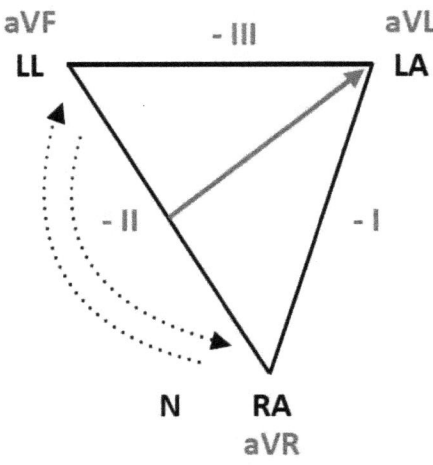
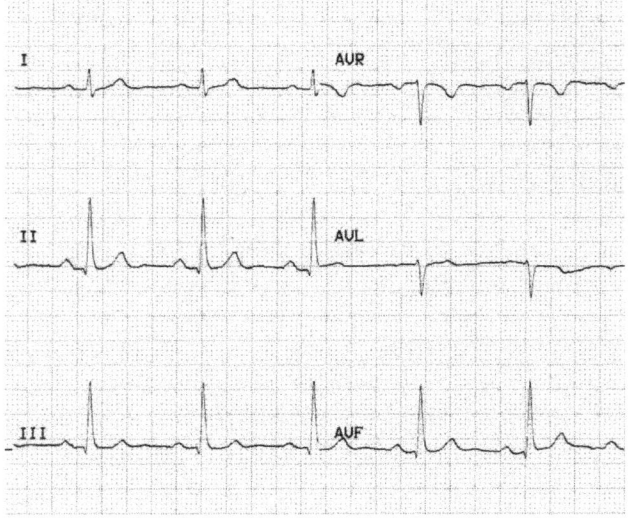

Dig. 1) Baseline ECG.
Dig. 2) RA/LL Reversal

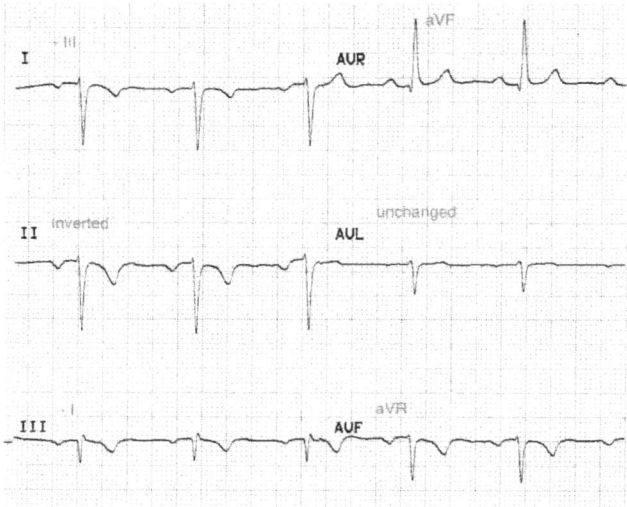

RA/RL (N) Reversal

With reversal of the RA and RL (N) Electrodes, Einthoven triangle collapses to very thin "slice" with the LA Electrode at its apex.

- The RA and LL Electrodes now record almost identical voltages, making the difference between them negligible (i.e. lead II = zero)

- Lead avL runs within this thin slice, facing approximately opposite to lead III.

- Displacement of the neutral electrode renders lead aVR and avF. Mathematically identical, such that they appear exactly alike (but different to the baseline ECG).

RA/RL (N) lead reversal has the following ECG features :-

- Lead I becomes an interval lead III
- Lead II records a flat line
- Lead III is unchanged
- Lead avL approximately an inverted lead III
- Lead aVR and avF become identical.

"Quick guide":- lead II is flat.

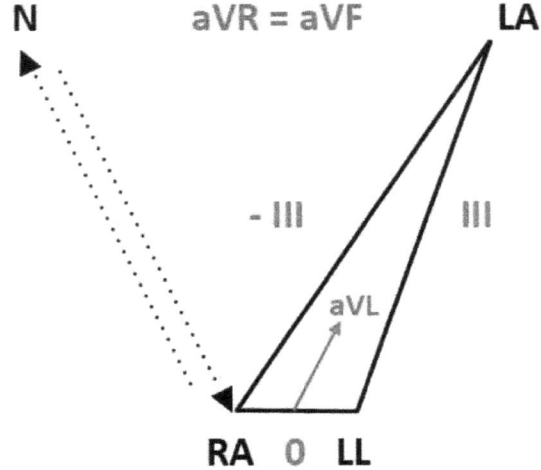

Rhythms

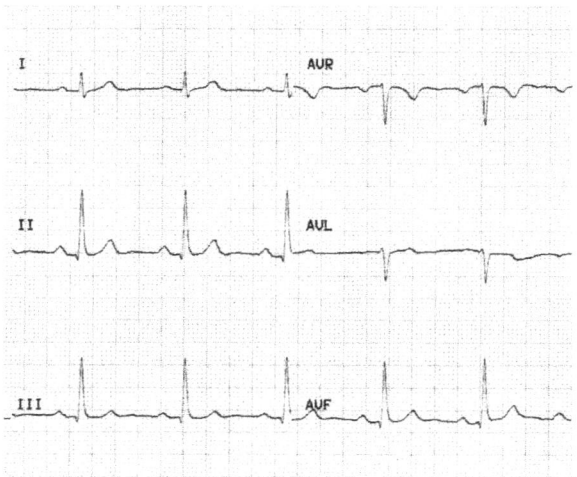

Dig. 1) Baseline ECG

Dig. 2) RA/RL Reversal

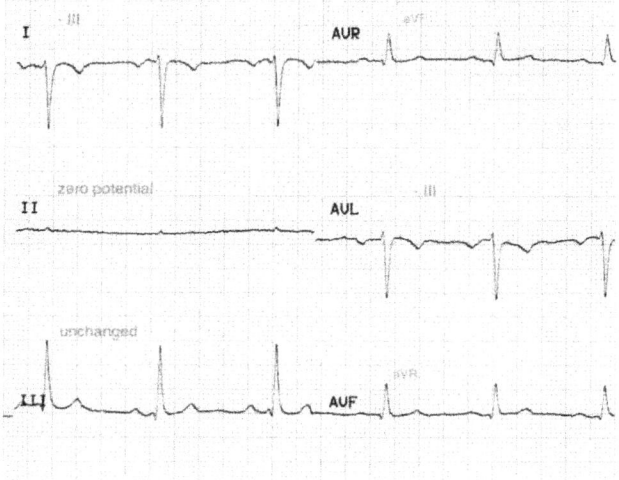

LA/RL (N) Reversal :-

With the reversal of the LA and RL (N) Electrodes Einthoven's triangle collapses to very thin "slice" with the RA Electrode at its Apex.

- The LA and LL Electrodes now record almost identical voltages, making the difference between them negligible (i,e lead III = zero)
- Lead aVR runs within this thin slice, facing approximately opposite to lead II.
- Displacement of the neutral Electrode renders lead avL, and avF mathematically identical such that they appear exactly alike.

LA/RL (N) lead reversal has the following ECG features

- Lead I becomes identical to lead II
- Lead II is unchanged
- Lead III records a flat line
- Lead aVR approximately to an inverted lead II
- Lead avL and avF become identical

"Quick guide" to spotting:- lead III is a flat line.

Rhythms

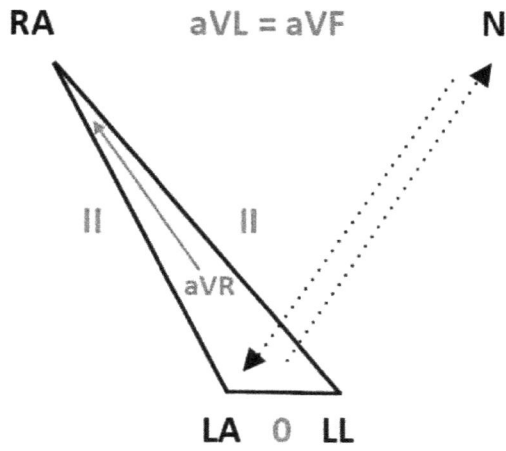

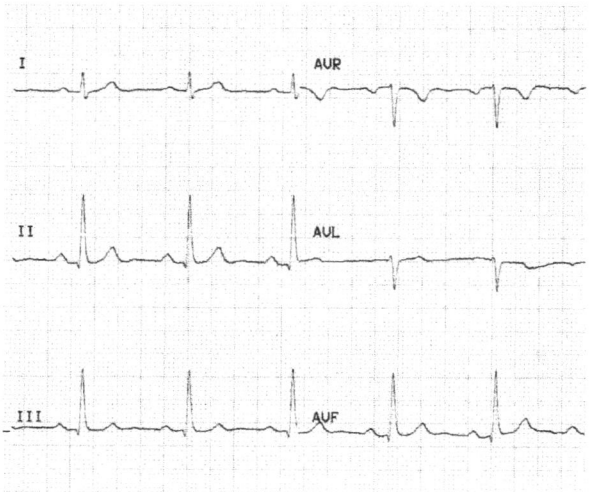

Dig. 1) Baseline ECG.

Dig. 2) LA/RL Reversal

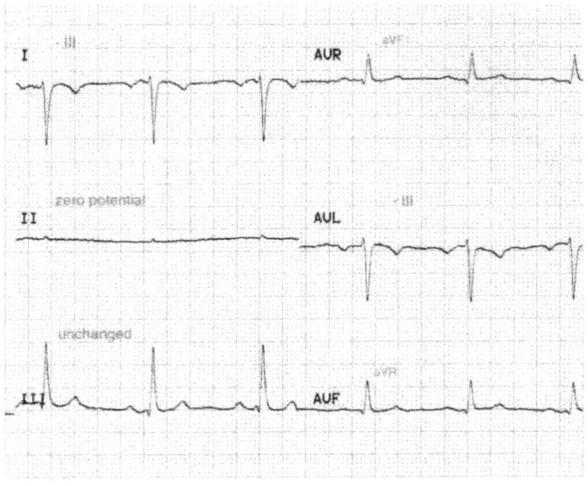

Bi – lateral Arm leg Reversal
[LA – LL Plus RA – RL]

If the Electrodes on each arm are swopped with their corresponding leg Electrode [LA with LL, RA with RL] Einthoven's Triangle collapses to very thin slice with the LL Electrode at its Apex.

- The RA and LA Electrodes record almost identical voltages, which makes the difference between them negligible (i,e lead I = zero).

- Lead II, III, aVR all become identical [Equivalent to interval lead III] as they are all now measuring the voltage difference between the left arm and the legs.

- Displacement of the neutral Electrode renders lead avL and aVR, mathematically identical such that they appear exactly alike.

Bi – lateral arm – leg reversal has the following ECG features:-

- Lead I records a flat line
- Lead II approximately an interval lead III.
- Lead III is inverted
- aVR and avL become identical
- avF looks like negative lead III.

"Quick guide" to spotting Bi- lateral Arm – leg reversal:-

- Lead I is a falt line.

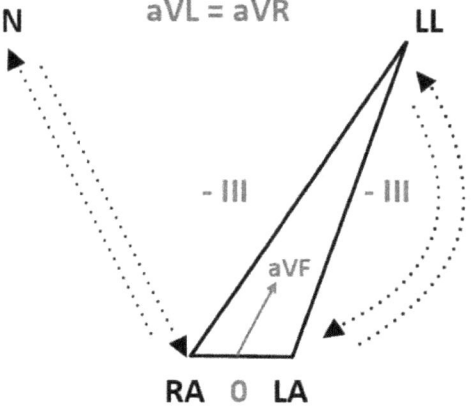

Bi – Lateral Arm – Leg Reversal

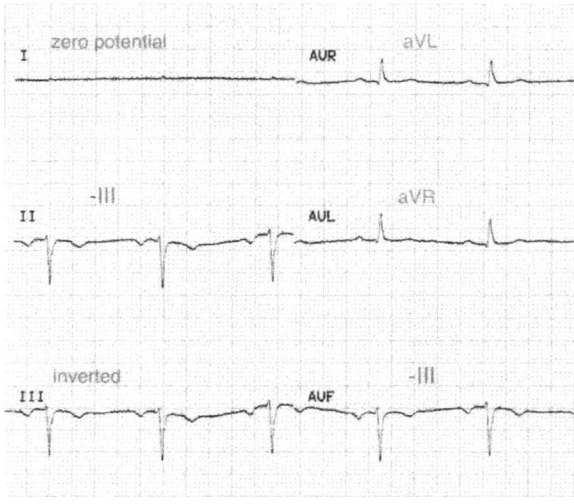

LL/RL (N) Reversal :-

With reversal of the lower limb Electrodes, Einthoven Triangle is preserved as the Electrical Signals from each leg are virtually identical.

Lead Reversal:- Left Arm/right Arm LA/RA reversal:-

With reversal of the LA/RA Electrodes, Einthoven's triangle flips 180 degree, horizontally around an Axis formed bylead avF.

This has the following effects on ECG :-

- Lead I becomes interted
- Lead II and III switch places
- Lead avL and aVR switch places
- Lead avF remains unchanged.

"Quick Guide":-

- Lead I is completely inverted
- Lead aVR often becomes positive
- There may be marked RAD.

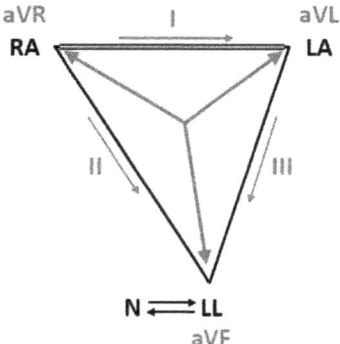

Left arm / Right arm Reversal

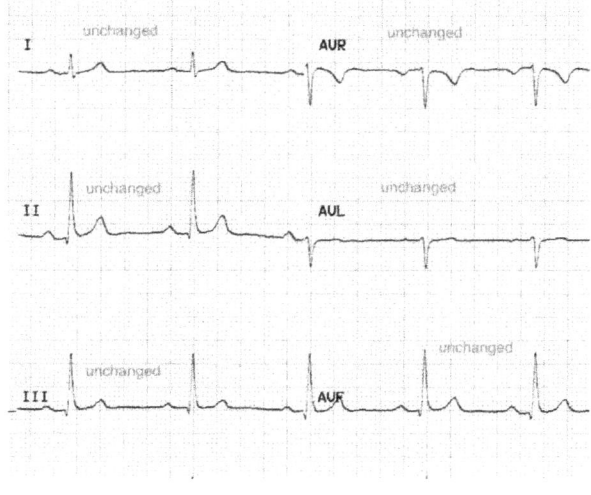

Sgarbossa Criteria Or Left Bundle Branch Block – Diagnosing Myocardial Infarction

In patients with left bundle branch block (LBBB) or ventricular paced rhythm, infarct diagnosis based on ECG is different.

- The baseline ST segment and T-waves tend to be shifted in a discordant direction, which can mask or mimic acute myocardial infarction.
- However, serial ECG's may show dynamic ST segment changes during ischaemia.
- A new LBBB is always pathological and can be sign of myocardial infarction
- First described by Elena B Sgarbossa in 1996.

Discordant ST-Segments and T-Waves

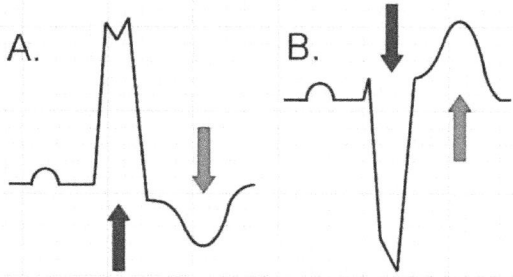

Normal for LBBB and paced rhythm

Original sgarbossa criteria :-

The original there criteria used to diagnose infarction in patients with LBBB are :-

- Concordant ST Elevation > 1mm in leads with a positive QRS complex (Score 5).

- Concordant ST depression > 1mm in v1 – v3 (score 3)

- Excessively Discordant ST elevation > 5mm in leads with negative QRS complex (score -2)

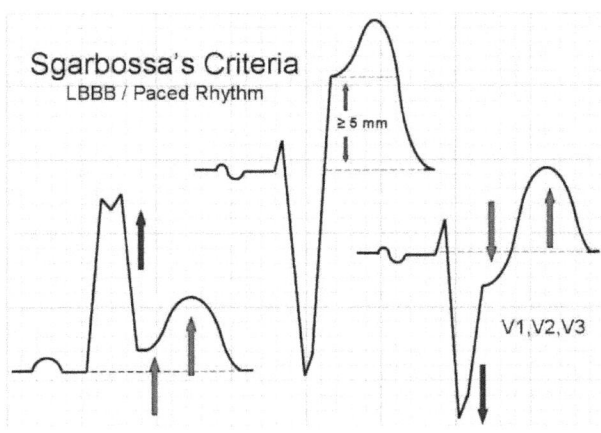

Modified sgarbossa criteria :-

As discussed in this article by Stephen smith modified sgarbossa criteria have been created to improve Dignostic accuracy the most important change is the modification of the rule for excessive Discordance.

The use of a 5mm cutoff For excessive discordance was arbitrary And non-specific for example, patients with LBBB and large voltage will commonly have ST deviations >5mm in the absence of ischaemia. The modified rule is positive for STEMI if there is discordant ST Elevation with amplitude >25% of depth of the preceding 'S'-wave.

Modified sgarbossa criteria:-

- ≥1 lead with ≥1mm of concordant ST Elevation.
- ≥1 lead of v1- v3 with ≥1mm of concordant ST depression.

- ≥1 lead anywhere with ≥1mm STE and proportionally Excessive Discordant STE, as defined by ≥25% of depth of the preceding S-wave.

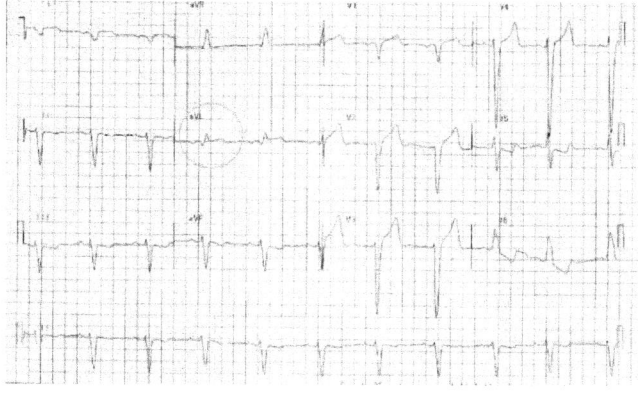

Pacemaker Malfunction

1) Pacemaker Malfunction Overview :-

Pacemaker malfunction can occur for a wide variety of reasons, ranging from equipment failure to changes in underlying native rhythm.

2) Diagnosis of Pacemaker: -

Malfunction is challenging and often associated with non – specific clinical symptoms while ECG changes can be subtle or absent.

Problems with Sensing Undersensing :-

1) Undersensing occurs when the pacemaker fails to sense native cardiac activity.
2) Results in asynchronous pacing.
3) Causesinclude increased simulation threshold at electrode site (exit block), poor lead contact, new bundle branch block or programming problems.
4) ECG findings may be minimal, although presence of pacing spikes within QRS complexes is suggestive of undersensing.

Oversensing :-
1) Oversensing occurs when electrical signals are inappropriately recognised as native cardiac activity nd pacing is inhibited.
2) These inappropriate signals may be large P or T waves, skeletal muscle activity or lead contact problems.
3) Abnormal signals may not be evident on ECG.
4) Reduced pacemaker output/output failure may be seen on ECG monitoring if the patient stimulates their rectus or pectoral muscles (due to oversensing of muscle activity).

ECG in Pacemaker Malfunction:-
1) Normal pacemaker rhythms can result in absent pacing activity, irregular pacing and absence of pacing spikes.
2) Diagnosis of pacemaker malfunction on the ECG is very difficult and may be impossible depending on the underlying native rhythm.
3) If pacemaker malfunction is suspected cardiology review is required to facilitate pacemaker interrogation and testing.

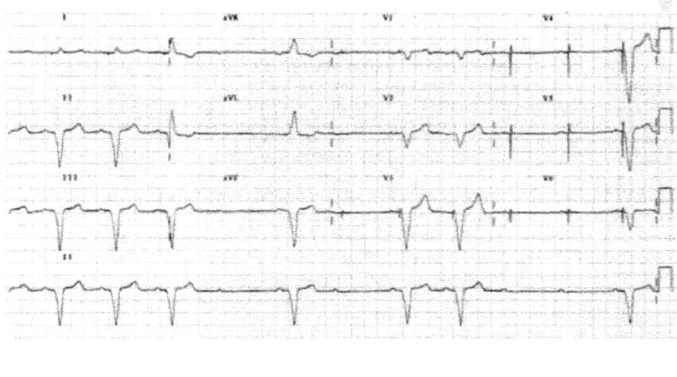

Atrial Tachycardia

Atrial Tachycardia Overview :-

Atrial tachycardia is a form of supraventricular tachycardia, originating within the atria but outside of the sinus node. Both atrial flutter and multifocal atrial tachycardia are specific types of atrial tachycardia.

ECG Features of Atrial Tachycardia :-

1) Atrial rate> 100bpm.
2) P- wave morphology is abnormal when compared with sinus P-wave due to ectopic origin.
3) There is usually an abnormal P-wave axis (e.g. inverted in the inferior leads II, III and aVF). At least three consecutive identical ectopic P-waves.
4) QRS complexes usually normal morphology unless pre-existing bundle branch block, accessory pathway, or rate related aberrant conduction.
5) Isoelectric baseline (unlike atrial flutter).
6) AV block may be present – this is generally a physiological response to the rapid atrial rate, except in the case of digoxin toxicity where there is actually AV node suppression due to the

vagotonic effects of digoxin, resulting in a slow ventricular rate ("PAT with block").

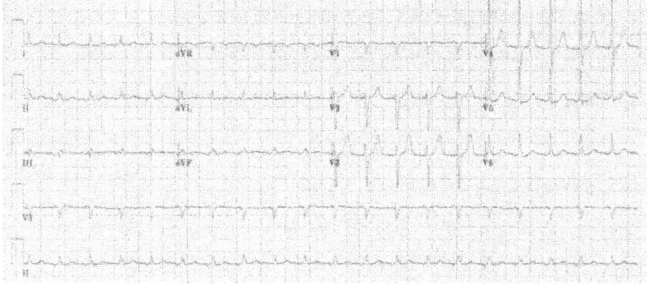

Left Ventricular Aneurysm

Left Ventricular Aneurysm Oberview :-

Persistent ST elevation following an acute myocardial infarction.

1) Following an acute STEMI, the ST segments return towards baseline over a period of two weeks, while the Q waves persist and the T-waves usually become flattened or inverted.

2) However, some degree of ST elevation remains in 60% of patients with anterior STEMI and 5% of patients with inferior STEMI.

3) The mechanism is thought to be related to incomplete reperfusion and transmural scar formation following an acute MI.

4) This ECG pattern is associated with paradoxical movement of the ventricular wall on echocardiography (ventricular aneurysm).

ECG Features of LV Aneurysm:-

1) ST elevation seen>2weeks following an acute myocardial infarction.

2) Most commonly seen in the precordial leads.

3) May exhibit concave or convex morphology.

4) Usually associated with well – formed Q- or QS waves.

5) T-waves have a relatively small amplitude in comparison to the QRS complex (unlike the hyperacute T-waves of acute STEMI).

Differentiation from acute STEMI:-

1) In patients presenting with chest pain and ST elevation on the ECG it is vital to be able to be distinguish between LV aneurysm ("old MI") and acute STEMI.

Factors favouring left ventricular aneurysm:
ECG identical to previous ECGs (if available). :-

1) Absence of dynamic ST segment changes.
2) Absence of reciprocal ST depression.
3) Well- formed Q-waves.

Factors favouring acute STEMI

1) New ST changes compared with previous ECGs.
2) Dynamic/progressive ECG changes – the degree of ST elevation increases on serial ECGs.
3) Reciprocal ST depression.
4) High clinical suspicion of STEMI – ongoing ischaemic chest pain, sick – looking patient (e.g. pale, sweaty), haemodynamic instability.

Anterior LV Aneurysm.

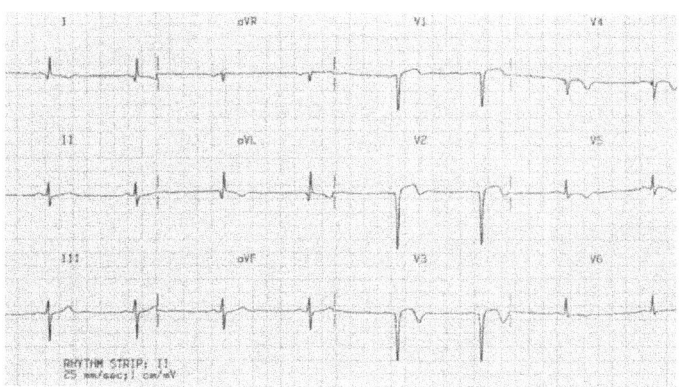

Inferior LV Aneurysm.

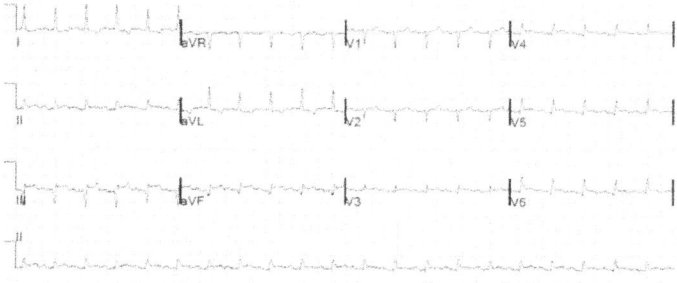

Paediatric ECG Interpretation

Paediatric ECG Interpretation :-

At birth, the right ventricle is larger and thicker than the left ventricle, reflecting the greater physiological stresses placed upon it in utero (I.e. pumping blood through the relatively high-resistance pulmonary circulation).

This produces an ECG picture reminiscent of right ventricular hypertrophy in the adult: marked rightward axis, dominant R-wave in V1 and T-wave inversion in V1-3.

Conduction intervals (PR interval, QRS duration) are shorter than adults due to the smaller cardiac size. Heart rates are much faster in neonates and infants, decreasing as the child grows older.

Common Findings on the Paediatric ECG

The following electrocardiographic features may be normal in children:

- Heart rate>100beats/min
- Rightward QRS axis> +90degree
- T-wave inversions in V1-3 ("juvenile T-wave pattern")
- Dominant R-wave in V1

- RSR' pattern in V1
- Marked sinus arrhythmia
- Short PR interval(<120ms) and QRS duration (<80ms)
- Slightly peaked P-waves(<3mm in height is normal if ≤6months)
- Slightly long QTc (≤490ms inn infants ≤6months)
- Q-waves in the inferior and left precordial leads.

Normal Paediatric ECG

ECG Incomplete RBBB Normal paediatric 2year old

This ECG of a healthy 2-year old boy displays many of the typical features of the paediatric ECG:

- Heart rate of 110 bpm (normal for age).
- Dominant R-waves in V1-3.
- RSR' pattern (partial RBBB morphology) in V1.
- Juvenile T-wave pattern (T-waves inversion in V1-3).

A Guide to Paediatric ECG Interpretation

The right ventricular dominance of the neonate and infant is gradually replaced by left ventricular dominance so that by 3-4 years the paediatric ECG resembles that of adults.

Content:-
1) Placement of ECG leads
2) Stepwise assessment of the ECG
3) Characteristic ECG patterns for particular conditions
4) Abnormal rhythms

Placement of ECG leads:- In young children, the right ventricle normally extends to the right side of the sternum. To appropriately display right ventricular potentials, ECGs for children in the under five-year age group must include an alternate lead ('V4R') on the right side of the chest at a point analogous to the left sided V4.

Precordial leads:-

V1: 4th intercostal space, right sternal border

V2: 4th intercostal space, left sternal border

V3: midway between V2 and where V4 would have been (5th intercostal space, left midclavicular line)

V4R: 5th intercostal space, right midclavicular line. Use this lead for V4R, must label as such on ECG.

V5: anterior axillary line, same horizontal plane as v4

V6: midaxillary line, same horizontal line as V4.

Limb leads:-

Place on top part of arm or leg (less muscle interference).

V4R ECG lead placement

Stepwise Assessment of the ECG
Rhythm

Sinus:- Atrial depolarisation starts from the sinoatrial node. This requires:

- P-wave preceding each QRS complex, with a constant PR interval.
- Normal P-wave axis (zero to +90degrees), I, e, P-wave is upright in leads I and aVF.

Non – sinus :- Some atrial rhythms may have P-waves in front of every QRS but with an abnormal P- axis (inverted in lead II).

Rate

Usual paper speed is 25mm/sec so 1mm (small square) =0, 04sec, and 5mm (big square) =0.2sec. Calculateatrial and ventricular rates separately if different. Many methods to estimate the rate, for **Example:-**

- For regular rhythms: 300/number of large squares in between each consecutive R-wave.
- For very fast rates: 1500/number of small squares in between each consecutive R-wave.
- For irregular rhythms: number of complexes on the rhythm strip×6.

Resting heart rate varies with age:-

- New born: 110 – 150bpm
- 2years: 85 – 125bpm
- 4years: 75 – 115bpm

- 6years : 60 – 100bpm

Ventricular rate is faster at baseline for younger children. The younger the child, the higher the metabolic rate and lower vegal tone, [O'Connor, 2008]

QRS axis

Calculated using the hexaxial reference system that shows the frontal view of the electrical activity of the heart via the six limb leads.

- Lead 1:- the R-wave represents the leftward force, the S-wave the rightward force.
- aVF:- the R-wave represents the downward force, the S-wave the upward force.

A suggested method of axis calculation Normal QRS axis varies with age:-

- 1 week – 1month: +110degree (range +30degree to +180degree)
- 1month – 3month: +70degree (range +10degree to +110degree)
- 3month – 3years: +60degree (range +20degree to +120degree)
- Over 3years: +60degree (range +20degree to +120degree)
- Adult: +50degree (range -30degree to 105degree)

Initial right ventricular (RV) dominance. In utero, blood is shunted away from the pulmonary vasculature lading to high pulmonary pressures and a relatively thick Right Ventricle (RV)

- Initial Right Axis on ECG is normal and resolves after the first 6 months of life
- An extreme superior Axis (Axis of -90 to -180 degreesis seen with AV canal oe osmium primum atrial septal defects.

ECG intervals
PR Interval :-

The normal PR interval varies with age and heart rate :

PR interval (ms) with age

Prolonged PR interval (first degree heart block) may be normal or be seen in :-

- Viral or rheumatic myocarditis and other myocardial dysfunctions.
- Certain congenital heart disease (Ebsteins, ECD, ASD)
- Digitalis toxicity
- Hyperkalaemia

Short PR interval occurs in :

- Pre – excitation (eg Wolff- Parkinson – White)
- Glycogen storage disease

Variable PR interval occurs in :

- Wandering atrial pacemaker
- Wenckebach (Mobitz type 1) second degree heart block

QRS Duration :-

QRS duration varies with age.

QRS duration (ms) with age prolonged QRS is characteristic of ventricular conduction disturbance.

- Bundle Branch blocks
- Pre-excitation conditions (eg WPW)
- Intraventricular block
- Ventricular arrhythmias

QT Interval :-

QT interval varies with heart rate :

Bazett formula is used to correct the QT for HR :

- QTC = QT measured/ ($\sqrt{}$R-R interval)

Normal QTc

- Infants less than 6 months = <0.49seconds
- Older than 6 months = <0.444seconds

QTC is prolonged in :

- Hypocalcaemia
- Myocarditis
- Long QT syndromes such as
- Romano – Ward
- Head injury
- Drugs

QTc is short in :
- Hypercalcaemia
- Digitalis effect
- Congenital short QT syndrome

P-wave amplitude and duration
- Normal P-wave amplitude is <3mm (tall P-waves = right atrial enlargement).
- Normal P-wave duration is <0.09seconds in children and <0.07seconds in infants (wide P-waves = left atrial enlargement).
- A combination of tall and wide P-waves occurs in combined atrial hypertrophy.

QRS amplitude (voltages)
High QRS amplitudes are found in:
- Ventricular hypertrophy
- Ventricular conduction disturbances eg, BBB's WPW

Low QRS amplitude are seen in :
- Pericarditis
- Myocarditis
- Hypothyroidism
- Normal new borns

Ventricular hypertrophy

Ventricular hypertrophy produces changes in one or more of the following areas: the QRS axis, the QRS voltages, the R/S ratio or the T-axis.

→R and S wave voltages children

Right ventricular hypertrophy Axis: RAD for the patients age

Voltages: Tall R-wave (greater than limits for patient's age) in right sided leads V4R and V1. Deep S-waves (greater than limits for patient's age) in left-sided leads V5 and V6.

R/S ratio: Abnormal R/S ratio in favour of RVH.

- Increased R/S ratio (greater than upper limits for child's age) in V1-2.
- R/S ratio <1 in V6 (after one month of age).

Abnormal T-waves: Upright T-waves in V1 and V4R in children 3days to 6years (provided that T-waves are normal elsewhere, i.e. upright in V6). This is evidence alone of significant RVH.

Abnormal Q-waves: qR pattern in V1 (small Q-wave, tall R-wave) = highly specific for RVH.

Left ventricular hypertrophy Axis. LAD for the patients age(marked LAD is rare with LVH).

Voltages: Tall R-waves in the left-sided leads V5 and V6 (greater than limits for patient's age). Deep S-waves in the right-sided leads V4R and V1 (greater than limits for patient's age).

R/S ratio :
- Abnormal R/S ratio in favour of LV
- Decreased R/S ratio in V1-2 (less than upper limits for child's age)

Abnormal Q-waves in V5 and V6

Inverted T-waves in I and aVL (LV strain pattern)

Bi-ventricular hypertrophy
- Positive voltages criteria for RVH and LVH (with normal QRS duration).
- Positive voltages criteria for RVH or LVH and relatively large voltages for other ventricle.
- Large equiphasic QRS complexes in two or more limb leads and in mid-precordial leads (V2-5).

Evans Rules :-

Small chest walls exaggerate precordial voltages. Evans et al proposed a practical approach to evaluation:

Abnormal Left Ventricular Large Voltage ("LVH")
- Use only V6 (the left most precordial lead).
- If R-wave of V6 intersects with baseline of V5, this is ABNORMAL

Abnormal Right Ventricular Large Volrage ("RVH")

Use only V1 (the right most precordial lead)

- Upright T-waves in V1: In first week of life is NORMAL. Between week 1 and adolescence this is ABNORMAL
- RSR' in V1: If R' is taller than R – this is ABNORMAL.
- Pure R-wave in V1: If child > 6months old – this is ABNORMAL

Q-Waves

Normal Q-waves :-

- Narrow (average 0.02seconds and less than 0.03 seconds).
- Usually less than 5mm deep in left precordial leads and aVF.
- May be as deep as 8mm in lead III in children younger than 3years.

Q-waves are abnormal if they:

- Appear in the right precordial leads ie V1 (eg severe RVH).
- Are absent in the left precordial leads (e.g. LBBB).
- Are abnormally deep (ventricular hypertrophy of the volume overload type).
- Are abnormally deep and wide (myocardial infarction or fibrosis).

ST segment

The normal ST is isoelectric. Elevation of depression is judged in relation to the TP segment.

Some ST changes may be normal:

- Limb lead ST depression or elevation of up to 1mm (up to 2mm in the left precordial leads).
- J-point depression: the J-point (junction between the QRS and ST segment) is depressed without sustaining ST depression, i.e. upsloping ST depression.
- Benign early repolarisation in adolescents: the ST segment is elevated and concave in leads with an upright T-wave.

Others are pathological:

- A downward slope of the ST followed by a biphasic inverted T.
- A sustained horizontal ST segment depression 0.08sec or longer.

Pathological ST segment changes are commonly associated with T-wave changes and occur in :

- Pericarditis
- Myocardial ischaemia or infarction.
- Severe ventricular hypertrophy (ventricular strain pattern).
- Digitalis effect

T-Waves

The precordial T-wave configuration changes over time.

- For the first week of life, T-waves are upright throughout the precordial leads.
- After the first week, the T-waves become inverted in V1-3 (=the "juvenile T-wave pattern")
- This T-wave inversion usually remains until ~ age 8; thereafter the T-waves become upright in V1-3.
- However, the juvenile T-wave pattern can persist into adolescence and early adulthood (= "persistent juvenile T-waves").

Tall, peaked T-waves are seen in:

- Hyperkalaemia
- LVH (volume overload)
- Benign early repolarisation

Flat T-waves are seen in:

- Normal new borns
- Hypothyroidism
- Hypokalaemia
- Digitalis
- Pericarditis
- Myocarditis

- Myocardial ischaemia

Large, deeply inverted T-waves are seen with:

- Raised intracranial pressure (e.g. intracranial haemorrhage, traumatic brain injury)

U-waves

U-waves are the extra positive deflection at the end of a T-wave.

Most common causes:

- Hypokalaemia.
- Normal U-wave adolescent ECG

Characteristic ECG pattern for particular conditions

ECG Abnormalities in children:

- Pericariditis (usually viral)
- Myocarditis (viral or rheumatic)
- Myocardial infarction (e.g. in children with anomalous coronary arteries / post - cardiac surgery / thrombophilla).
- Hypocalaemia/hypercalcaemia.
- Hypokalaemia/hyperkalaemia.
- Wolff-Parkinson-White syndrome (see "Abnormal Rhythms" section below)

Pericarditis

Pericardial effusion may produce QRS voltages less than 5mm in all limb leads. Sub – epicardial myocardial damage causes time dependant change:

- Initial widespread concave ST segment elevation and PR segment depression.
- ST segment returns to normal within 1-3 weeks, elevation and PR segment depression.
- T-wave inversion (with isoelectric ST segment) occurs from 2-4 weeks after the onset of pericarditis.

Myocarditis

ECG findings of rheumatic or viral myocarditis are relatively non-specific and may include:

- AV conduction disturbances, ranging from PR prolongation to complete AV dissociation.
- Low QRS voltages (5mm or less in all limb leads).
- Decreased T-wave amplitude.
- QT prolongation.
- Tachyarrhythmias including SVT and VT.
- 'Pseudoinfarction' pattern with deep Q-waves and poor R-wave progression in precordial leads.

NB. Prolonged PR interval is a minor Jones criteria for acute rheumatic fever.

Myocardial infarction/ischaemia

The appearance are normally identical to those seenin adult ischaemia or infarction.

- Infarction: ST elevation in contiguous leads with reciprocal ST depression elsewhere.
- Ischaemia : Horizontal ST depression.

Calcium abnormalities

- Hypocalcaemia prolongs the ST segment with resulting prolongation of the QTc.
- Hypercalcaemia shortens the ST segment and the QTc.

The T-wave is relatively unaffected in both conditions.

ECG-QT-changes-Hypocalcaemia-Hypercalcaemia

Potassium abnormalities

Hypokalaemia

With K+ <2.5 mmol/L:

- Prominent U-waves develop with apparent prolongation of the QTc (prolonged "QU" interval)
- Flat or biphasic T-waves
- ST segment depression

As K + falls further:

- PR interval prolongs.
- Sinoatrial block may occur.

Hyperkalaemia

As K + rises (>6.0mmol/L)

- Tall peaked T-waves, best seen in precordial leads.
- Prolongation of QRS duration.
- Prolongation of PR interval.
- Disappearance of P-waves.
- Wide bizarre biphasic QRS complexes (sine waves).
- Eventual asystole.

Abnormal Rhythms
Supraventricular Tachycardia (SVT)

Characteristic of SVT

- Rapid regular, usually narrow (<80ms) complex tachycardia of 220 – 320bpm in infants and 150 – 250 in older children.
- The P-wave is usually invisible, or if visible is abnormal in axis and may precede or follow the QRS ("retrograde P-waves").
- 90% of paediatric dysrhythmias are SVT; 90% of SVT are of re-entrant type.
- Half of patients with SVT will have no underlying heart disease.
- Consider fever or drug exposure (particularly sympathimimetics).

- Almost ¼ will have congenital heart disease and ¼ will have WPW.

- SVT may be well tolerated in infants for 12 – 24hours.Congestive heart failure later manifests with irritability, poor perfusion, pallor, poor feeding and then rapid deterioration.

- Note that >95% of wide complex tachycardias in paediatrics are NOT VT, but SVT with aberrancy, SVT with BBB (in pre-existing congenital heart disease) or a type of accessory pathway re-entrant SVT (see below).

- Do NOT use verapamil or beta blockres in infants or children with SVT – may cause profound AV block, negative inotropy and sudden death.

SVT at ~250bpm (the RSR' pattern in V1 is normal finding in children)

Types of Supraventricular tachycardia (SVT)

Supraventricular tachycardia comprises two main types:

1) Re-entrant SVT
2) Automatic SVT

1) Re-entrant SVT:-

- This comprises the majority of SVT (90%).
- HR doses not vary substantially in re-entrant tachycardia.
- Typically begins and ends abruptly.

Mechanisms:-

Requires bypass pathway between atria and ventricles in addition to the AV node. Bypass pathway can be either an anatomically separate accessory pathway (the Bundle of Kent as in most cases of Wolf – Parkinson – White) or a functionally separate pathway within the AV node (called AV nodal re-entry tachycardia).

For SVT to occur the two pathways must have at least, temporarily, different conduction and recovery rates. A circular rhythm down one path and up the other begins when an atrial or ventricular contrction finds one pathway able to conduct while the other is temporarily refractory.

If the second path is able to conduct by the time the impulse has passed through the AV node, it may conduct the opposite direction; thus, setting up a re-entry tachycardia.

The ECG findings will very according to the type of bypass tract (anatomic or functional) and the direction of the impulse flow through the AV node (atrium to ventricle, or visa versa).

The presence of AV block will interrupt any re-entrant tachycardia that involves the AV node; therefore adenosine (transiently blocks AV conduction) works well for these rhythms. Several atrial rhythms; atrial flutter, atrial fibrillation and sinoatrial node re-entry tachycardia are also considered subgroups of re-entrant SVT. These do not respond to adenosine but the transient slowing of the ventricular rate may unmask the atrial activity and therefore underlying cause of the SVT. A running rhythm strip is therefore imperative.

Wolff-Parkinson-White Syndrome

WPW syndrome is characterised by the occurrence of SVT plus specific ECG findings in sinus rhythm. The characteristic pre-excitation is evidenced by a short PR interval and widened QRS with a slurred upstroke or delta wave.

It is caused by earlier ventricular excitation occurring via the accessory pathway than have occurred via the normal AV node alone. With the onset of SVT, conduction reverses (becomes V to A) in the accessory pathway as part of the circular rhythm.

In small number of patients with WPW, accessory pathway conduction is A to V in SVT (and reversed to become V to A in the AV node). This results in an anomalous ventricular activation sequence and a wide complex QRS (>120msec) and followed by retrograde P-waves which may be difficult to differentiate from VT

2) Automatic SVT

SVT due to abnormal or accelerated normal automatically (e.g. sympathomimetics). Usually accelerate ("warm up") and decelerate ('cool down') gradually.

- Sinus tachycardia: enhanced automatic rhythm. Rate varies with physiological state.

- Atrial tachycardia: non-reciprocating or ectopic atrial tachycardia – rapid firing of a single focus in the atria. Slower heart rate (130 – 160). Rare. Usually, constant rather than paroxysmal.
- Junctional Ectopic Tachycardia: difficult to treat, usually occurs in setting of post extensive atrial surgery. Rapid firing of a single focus in the AV node. Slower rhythm- 120 – 200bpm.

Anterior Myocardial Infarction

Clinical Relevance of Anterior Myocardial Infarction

Anterior STEMI results from occlusion of the left anterior decending artery (LAD). Anterior myocardial infarction carries the worst prognosis of all infarct locations, mostly due to larger infarct size.

A study comparing outcomes from anterior and inferior infarctions (STEMI + NSTEMI) found that on average, patients with anterior MI had higher incidences of in-hospital mortality (11.9 vs 2.8%), total morality (27 vs 11%), heart failure (41 vs 15%) and significant ventricular ectopic activity (70 vs 59 %) and a lower ejection fraction on admission (38 vs 55%) compared to patients with inferior MI.

In addition to anterior STEMI, other high-risk presentations of anterior ischaemia include left main coronary artery (LMCA) occlusion, Wellens syndrome and De Winter T-waves.

How to Recognise Anterior STEMI:-

- ST segment elevation with Q-wave formation in the precordial leads (V1-6) ± the high lateral leads (I and aVL.)

- Reciprocal ST depression in the inferior leads (mainly III and aVF).

Patterns of Anterior Infarction :-

The nomenclature of anterior infarction can be confusing, with multiple different terms used for the various infarction patterns. The following is a simplified approach to naming the different types of anterior MI.

The precordial leads can be classified as follows:

- Septal leads = V1-2
- Anterior leads = V3-4
- Lateral leads = V5-6

The different infarct patterns are named according to the leads with maximal ST elevation:

- Septal = V1-2
- Anterior = V2-5
- Anteroseptal = V1-4
- Anterolateral = V3-6, I +aVL
- Extensive anterior/anterolateral = V1-6, I + aVL

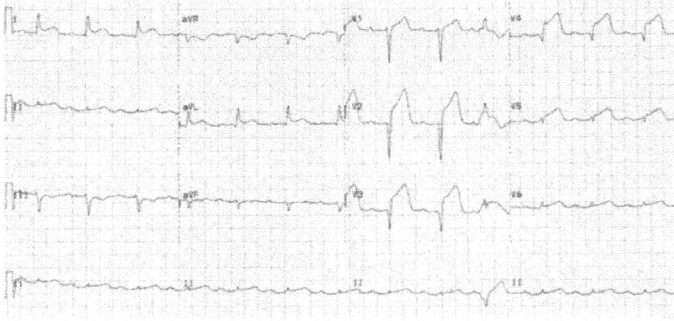

Clinical Pearls

Other important ECG patterns to be aware of:

- Anterior – inferior STEMI due to occlusion of a "wraparound" LAD simultaneous ST elevation in the precordial and inferior leads due to occlusion of a variant ("type III") LAD that wraps around the cardiac apex to supply both the anterior and inferior walls of the left ventricle.

- Left main coronary artery occlusion: widespread ST depression with ST elevation in aVR ≥ V1

- Wellens syndrome: deep precordial T-wave inversions or biphasic T-waves in V2-3, indicating critical proximal LAD stenosis (a warming sign of imminent anterior infarction)

- De Winter T-waves: upsloping ST depression with symmetrically peaked T-waves in the precordial leads; a "STEMI equivalent" indicating acute LAD occlusion.

Prediction of the Site of LAD Occlusion

The site of LAD occlusion (proximal versus distal) predicts both infarct size and prognosis.

- Proximal LAD/LMCA occlusion has a significantly worse prognosis due to larger infarct size and more severe haemodynamic disturbance.

- The site of occlusion can be inferred from the pattern of ST changes in leads corresponding to the two most proximal branches of the LAD: the first septal branch (S1) and the first diagonal branch (D1)

Territories

- S1 supplies the basal part of the interventricular septum, including the bundle branches (corresponding to leads aVR and V1)
- D1 supplies the high lateral region of the heart (leads I and aVL).

Occlusion proximal to S1

Signs of basal septal involvement:

- ST elevation in aVR
- ST elevation in V1 > 2.5mm
- Complete RBBB
- ST depression in V5

Occlusion proximal to D1

Signs of high lateral involvement:

- ST elevation/Q-wave formation in aVL
- ST depression $\geq$ 1mm in II, III or aVF (reciprocal to STE in aVL)

Rhythms

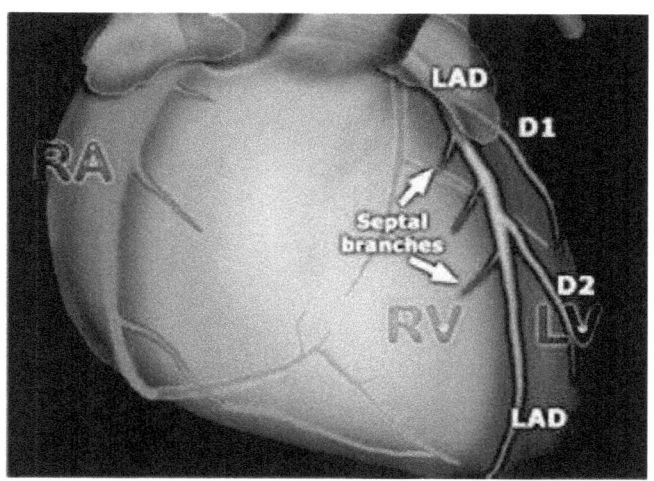

Lateral Stemi

Definitions :-

- ST elevation primarily localized to leads I and aVL is reffered to as a high lateral STEMI

- It is usually associated with reciprocal ST depression and T-wave inversion in the inferior leads.

- Sometimes referred to as the South African Flag sign

ECG High Lateral STEMI

Culprit vessels

Occlusion of the first diagonal branch (D1) of the left anterior descending artery (LAD) may produce isolated ST elevation in I and Avl Occlusion of the circumflex artery may cause ST elevation in I, aVL along with leads V5-6.

South African Flag sign

High lateral STEMI is associated with pattern of ST elevation caused by acute occlusion of the first diagonal branch of the left anterior descending coronary artery (LAD –D1)

With the 4×3 display of the 12-lead ECG, the location of the most impressive ST deviation resemble the shape of the South African flag.

- ST Elevation: Lead I, aVL, V2
- ST Depression: Lead III (and inferior leads)

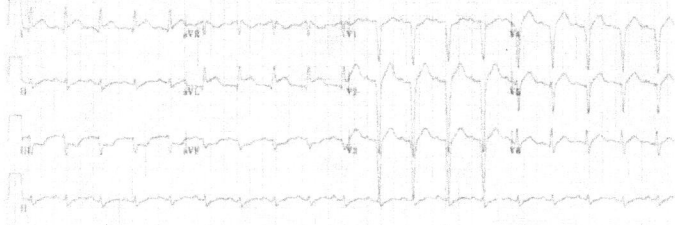

Inferior Stemi

Inferior ST Elevation Myocardial Infarction

Inferior MI accounts for 40-50% of all myocardial infarctions.

- Generally, have a more favourable prognosis than anterior myocardial infarction (in hospital mortality only 2-9%), however certain factors indicate a worse outcome.

- Up to 40% of patients with an inferior STEMI will have a concomitant right ventricular infarction. These patients may develop severe hypotension inresponse to nitrates and generally have a worse prognosis.

- Up to 20% of patients with inferior STEMI will develop significant bradycardia due to second or third-degree AV block. These Patients have an increased in hospital mortality (>20%).

- Inferior STEMI may also be associated with posterior infarction, which confers a worse prognosis due to increased area of myocardium at risk.

How to recognise an inferior STEMI

- ST elevation in leads II, III and aVF progressive development of Q-waves in II, III and aVF
- Reciprocal ST depression in aVL (± lead I)

Which Artery is the Culprit?

Inferior STEMI can result from occlusion of all three coronary arteries:

- The vast majority (~80%) of inferior STEMIs are due to occlusion of the dominant right coronary artery (RCA).
- Less commonly (around 18% of the time), the culprit vessel is a dominant left circumflex artery (LCx).
- Occasionally, inferior STEMI may result from occlusion of a "type III" or "wraparound" left anterior descending artery (LAD). This produces the unusual pattern of concomitant inferior and interior ST elevation.

While both RCA and circumflex occlusion may cause infarction of the interior wall, the precise area of infarction in each case is slightly different:

- The RCA territory covers the medial part of the inferior wall, including the inferior septum.
- The LCx territory covers the lateral part of the inferior wall and the left posterobasal area.

This produces subtly different patterns on the ECG:

- The injury current in RCA occlusion is directed inferiorly and rightward, producing ST elevation in lead III > lead II (as lead III is more rightward facing).
- The injury current in LCx occlusion is directed inferiorly and leftward, producing ST elevation in lateral lead I and V5-6.

These differences allow for electrocardiographic differentiation between RCA and LCx occlusion.

RCA occlusion is suggested by:

- ST elevation in lead III > lead II
- Presence of reciprocal ST depression in lead I
- Signs of right ventricular infarction: STE in V1 and V4R

Circumflex occlusion is suggested by:

- ST elevation in lead II = Lead III
- Absence of reciprocal ST depression in lead I
- Signs of lateral infarction: ST elevation in the lateral leas I and aVL or V5-6

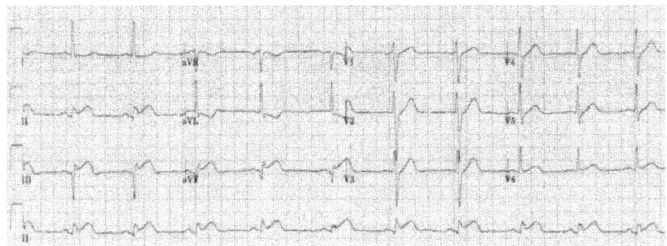

Posterior Myocardial Infarction

Clinical significance of posterior MI

Posterior infarction accompanies 15-20% of STEMIs, usually occurring in the context of an inferior or lateral infarction.

- Isolated posterior MI is less common (3-11% of infarcts).
- Posterior extension of an inferior or lateral infarct implies a much larger area of myocardial damage, with an increased risk of left ventricular dysfunction and death.
- Isolated posterior infarction is an indication of emergent coronary reperfusion. However, the lack of obvious ST elevation in this condition means that the diagnosis is often missed.

Be vigilant for evidence of posterior MI in any patient with an inferior or lateral STEMI.

How to spot posterior infarction

As the posterior myocardium is not directly visualised by the standard 12-lead ECG, reciprocal changes of STEMI are sought in the anteroseptal leads V1-3.

Posterior MI is suggested by the following changes in V1-3:

- Horizontal ST depression.
- Tall, broad R-waves (>30ms)
- Upright T-waves
- Dominant R-waves (R/S ratio>1) in V2

Explanation of the ECG changes in V1-3

The anteroseptal leads are directed from the anterior precordium towards the internal surface of the posterior myocardium. Because posterior electrical activity is recorded from the anterior side of the heart, the typical injury pattern of ST elevation and Q-waves become inverted:

- ST elevation becomes ST depression
- Q-waves becomes R-waves
- Terminal T-wave inversion becomes an upright T-wave

The progressive development of pathological R-waves in posterior infarction (the "Q-wave equivalent") mirrors the development of Q-waves in anteroseptal STEMI.

Posterior leads

Leads V7-9 are placed on the posterior chest wall in the following positions (see the diagram below)

- V7 – Left posterior axillary line, in the same horizontal plane as V6.
- V8 – Tip of the left scapula, in the same horizontal plane as V6.

- V9 – Left paraspinal region, in the same horizontal plane as V6.

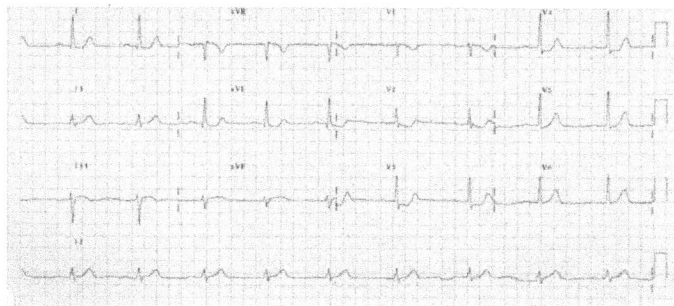

Right Ventricular Infarction

Clinical Significance of RV infarction

Right ventricular infarction complicates up to 40% of inferior STEMIs. Isolated RV infarction is extremely uncommon.

Patients with RV infarction are very preload sensitive (due to poor RV contractility) and can develop severe hypotension in response to nitrates or other preload-reducing agents.

Hypotension in right ventricular infarction is treated with fluid loading, and nitrates are contraindicated.

How to spot right ventricular infarction

The first step to spotting RV infarction is to suspect it... in all patients with inferior STEMI!

In patients presenting with inferior STEMI, right ventricular infarction is suggested by the presence of :

- ST elevation inV1 – the only standard ECG lead that looks directly at the ventricle.

- ST elevation in lead III> Lead II – because lead III is more "rightward facing" than lead II and hence more sensitive to the injury current produced by the right ventricle.

Other useful tips for spotting right ventricular MI:

- ST elevation in V1 > V2.
- ST elevation in V1 + ST depression in V2 (=highly specific for RV MI).
- Isoelectric ST segment in V1 with marked ST depression in V2.

Right ventricular infarction is confirmed by the presence of ST elevation in the right – sided leads (V3R-V6R).

Right-sided leads

There are several approaches to recording a right-sided ECG :

- A complete set of right-sided leads is obtained by placing leads v1-6 in a mirrior-image position on the right side of the chest (see diagram below).
- It may be simpler to leave V1 and V2 in their usual positions and just transfer leads V3-6 to the right side of the chest (I.e. V3R to V6r).
- The most useful lead inV4R, which is obtained by placing the V4 electrode in the 5th right intercostal space in the midclavicular line.
- ST elevation in V4R has a sensitivity of 88%, specificity of 78% and diagnostic accuracy of 83% in the diagnosis of RV MI.

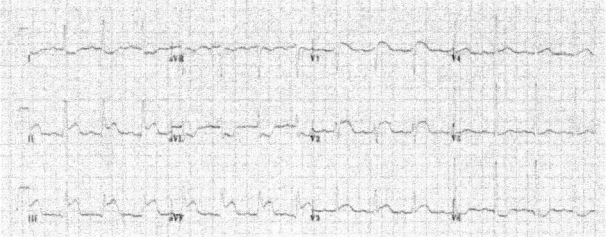

Takotsubo Cardiomyopathy

Takotsubo Cardiomyopathy Overview

A STEMI mimic producing ischaemic chest pain. ECG changes +/- elevated cardiac enzymes with characteristic regional wall motion abnormalities on echocardiography.

- Typically occurs in the context of severe emotional distress ("broken heart syndrome").
- Patients have normal coronary arteries on angiography.
- Originally described in Japan within the last 20 years, Tako-tsubo has become increasingly recognised, possibly in no small part due to the increased use of angiography in cardiology.

Diagnosis:-

Mayo Clinic criteria for takotsubo cardiomyopathy (widely but not universally accepted)

- New ECG changes (ST elevation or T-wave inversion) or moderate troponin rise.

- Transient akinesis/dyskinesis of left ventricle (apical and mid-ventricular segments) with regional wall abnormalities extending beyond a signal vascular territory.

- Absence of coronary artery stenosis >50% or culprit lesion.

Why Is It Called Takotsubo Cardiomyopathy?

The left ventricle, with its apical akinesia looks remarkably like a basket used in Japan to catch Octopi.

What Causes Tako-Tsubo?

Classically it occurs in a post-menopausal woman experiencing sudden emotional stress associated with a Cathecholamine Surge.

- Microvascular Spasm.
- Sympathetic nervous system activation.
- Underlying LVOTO.

A sudden surge in cathecholamines is agreed to be the cause, but the reason why this surge causes a characteristic wall motion abnormality remains a matter for debate.

The most widely held view is that the catecholamines cause micerovscular spasm, although left ventricular outflow obstruction is likely to play a part.

The sympathetic nervous system is also implicated – the condition can beprevented in a laboratory by cardiac sympathectomy, the apical distribution explained as it has the highest density of sympathetic nerve fibres.

Similar cardiac histopathological features are seen in patients who've had a subarachnoid haemorrhage.

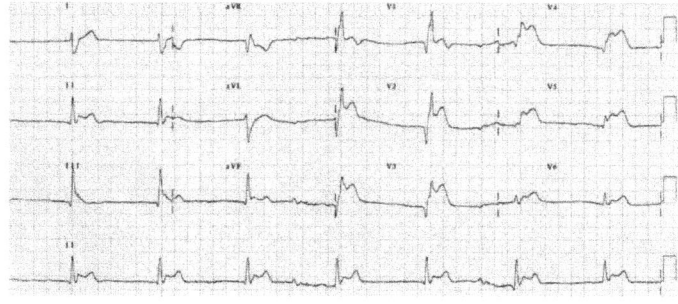

LMCA Occlusion: ST Elevation In AVR

Left main coronary artery (LMCA) Overview

Typical ECG findings with LMCA occlusion:

- Widespread horizontal ST depression, most prominent in leads I, II and V4-6
- ST elevation in aVR ≥1mm
- ST elevation in aVR ≥V1

ST Elevation in aVR

NOTE: - ST elevation in aVR is not entirely specific to LMCA occlusion.

ST Elevation in aVR may also be seen with :

- Proximal left anterior descending artery (LAD) occlusion
- Severe triple-vessel disease (3VD)
- Diffuse subendocardial ischaemia – e.g. due to 02 supply/demand mismatch, following resuscitation from cardiac arrest

Mechanism of ST elevation (STE) in aVR

- Lead aVR is electrically opposite to the left-sided leads I, II aVL and V4-6; therefore, ST depression in these leads will produce reciprocal ST elevation in aVR.

- Lead aVR also directly records electrical activity from the right upper portion of the heart, including the right ventricular outflow tract and the basal portion of the interventricular septum. Infarction in this area could theoretically produce ST elevation in aVR.

Cause of ST elevation (STE) in aVR

Two possible mechanisms:-

- Diffuse subendocardial ischaemia, with ST depression in the lateral leads producing reciprocal change in aVR (=most likely).

- Infarction of the basal septum, i.e. a STEMI involving aVR.

The basal septum is supplied by the first septal perforator artery (a very proximal branch of the LAD), so ischaemia/infarction of the basal septum would imply involvement of the proximal LAD or LMCA.

Predictive Valve of STE in aVR

In the context of widespread ST depression + symptoms of myocardial ischaemia :

- STE in aVR ≥1mm indicates proximal LAD/LMCA occlusion or severe 3VD

- STE in aVR ≥1mm predicts the need of CABG

- STE in aVR ≥V1 differentiates LMCA from proximal LAD occlusion
- Absence of ST elevation in aVR almost entirely excludes a significant LMCA lesion

In the context of anterior STEMI :
- STE in aVR ≥ 1mm is highly specific for LAD occlusion proximal to the first septal branch

In patients undergoing exercise stress testing :
- STE of ≥1mm in aVR during exercise stress testing predicts LMCA or ostial LAD stenosis

Magnitude of ST elevation in aVR is correlated with mortality in patients with acute coronary syndromes:

- STE in aVR ≥ 0.5mm was associated with a 4-fold increase in mortality
- STE in aVR ≥ 1mm was associated with a 6-to 7- fold increase in mortality
- STE in aVR ≥ 1.5mm has been associated with mortalities ranging from 20-75%.

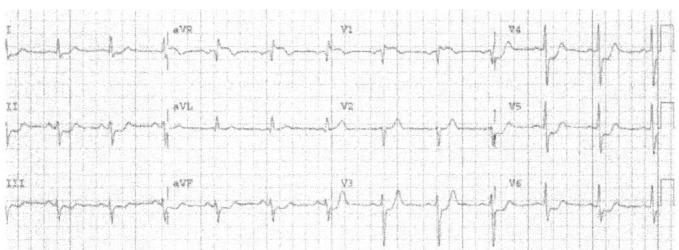

Misplacement Of V1 And V2

Misplacement of V1 and V2 : Don't let this mistake mess up your ECG interpretation!

The proper location of V1 and V2 have not changed in many decades. They are located in the 4th intercostal space, just right and left, respectively, of the sternum. It is fairly easy to determine this spot using the angle of Louis as a landmark.

However, V1 and V2 were being misplaced pretty much right after being invested. This error in lead positioning usually produces trivial changes in the QRS pattern in those leads, and thus no real change in ECG interpretation. But certain erroneous ECG patterns can be generated, and it is important to recognize lead misplacement as a potential cause.

Recognizing misplacement of V1 and V2

P-wave changes

In the vast majority of healthy patients, V1 will have a biphasic P-wave, while V2 will be upright. Upwards misplacement should be strongly suspected if the P in V1 is fully negative, or if the P in V2 is biphasic or fully negative. (If the leads are properly placed, consider e.g. atrial enlargement or an ectopic atrial rhythm.)

Incomplete Right Bundle Branch Block (rSr' pattern)

Upward misplacement of V1 and V2 often produces an IRBBB pattern.

IRBBB is a normal finding, seen in healthy athletes and children. However, a falsely "new" IRBBB might prompt the unwary clinician to consider pulmonary embolism, among other diagnoses.

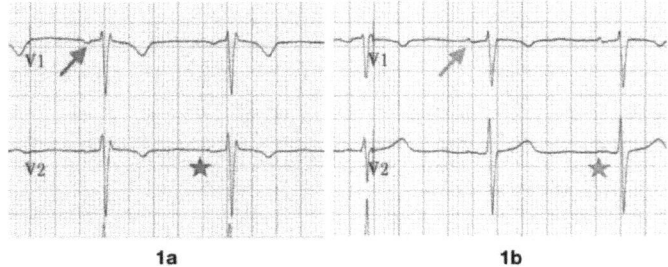

Old "Septal MI"

Seemingly new Q-waves can be generated with high placement of V1 and V2. If there is supporting clinical context, an old septal MI can be considered, and confirmatory labs and imaging obtained. Otherwise, the ECG should be scrutinized for the signs of misplacement and repeated.

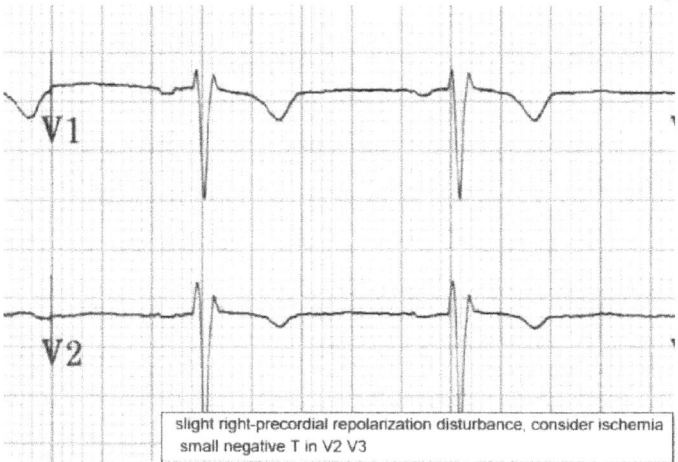

slight right-precordial repolarization disturbance, consider ischemia
small negative T in V2 V3

False STEMI

In some cases, the rSr' or qR pattern may combine with a mild degree of benign anterior ST segment elevation (aka "male pattern"). This produces a "saddle-shaped" ST segment that the computer may mistake for acute ischaemia.

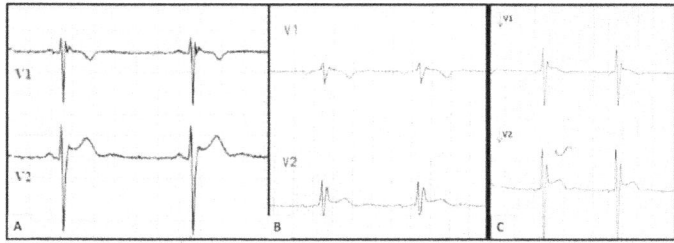

T-wave inversion

T-wave inversion may be normal in V1 and V1. However, in patients with symptoms that suggest a cardiopulmonary cause, an inverted T-wave must be presumed to be pathologic. Upwards misplacement of V2 can generate false T-wave inversion

Brugada – Type 2 (Not Type 1)

V1 and V2 may be placed in the 3rd or even 2nd intercostal spaces in order to elicit a type 1 Brugada pattern, and is considered diagnostic.

By contrast, a type 2 brugada pattern may often be found with these "high leads" are applied to healthy people, especially in fit young males. Finding type 2 Brugada in this context is not uncommon, and by itself carries no diagnostic or prognostic significance.

A number of the examples above show a pattern that could be mistaken for type 2 Brugada.

Idiopathic Fascicular Left Ventricular Tachycardia

Overview

- Fascicular tachycardia is the most common idiopathic VT of the left ventricle.
- It is re-entrant tachycardia, typically seen in young patients without structural heart disease.
- Verapamil is the first line treatment.

AKA:- Fascicular tachycardia, Belhssen-type VT, verapamil-sensitive VT or infrafascicular tachycardia.

Idiopathic VT

- Only 10% of cases of VT occur in the absence of structural heart disease, termed idiopathic VT.
- The majority of idiopathic VTs (75-90%) arise from theright ventricle – e.g. right ventricular outflow tract tachycardia.
- Fascicular VT is the most common type of idiopathic VT arising from the left ventricle (10-15% of all idiopathic VTs).

Causes

Usually occurs in young healthy patients (15-40years of age; 60-80% male). Most episodes occur at rest but may be triggered by exercise, stress and beta agonists. The mechanism is re-entrant tachycardia due to an ectopic focus within the left ventricle.

NB. A similar ECG pattern of fascicular VT may occur with digoxin toxicity, but here the mechanism is the enhanced automatically in the region of the fascicles.

ECG Features of Idiopathic Fascicular Left Ventricular Tachycardia

- Monomorphic ventricular tachycardia eg. Fusion complexes, AV dissociation, capture beats.
- QRS duration 100-400ms – this is narrower than forms of VT.
- Short RS interval (onset of R to nadir of S-wave) of 60-80ms – the RS interval is usually >100ms in other types of VT.
- RBBB Pattern
- Axis deviation depending on anatomical site of re-entry circuit (see classification)

Classification

Fascicular tachycardia can be classified based on ECG morphology corresponding to the anatomical location of the re-entry circuit:

1) Posterior fascicular VT (90-95% of cases): RBBB morphology + left axis deviation; arises close to the left posterior fascicle.
2) Anterior fascicular VT (5-10% of cases): RBBB morphology + right axis deviation; arises close to the left anterior fascicle.
3) Upper septal fascicular VT (rare): a typical morphology – usually RBBB but may resemble LBBB instead; cases with narrow QRS and normal axis have also been reported. Arises from the region of the upper septum.

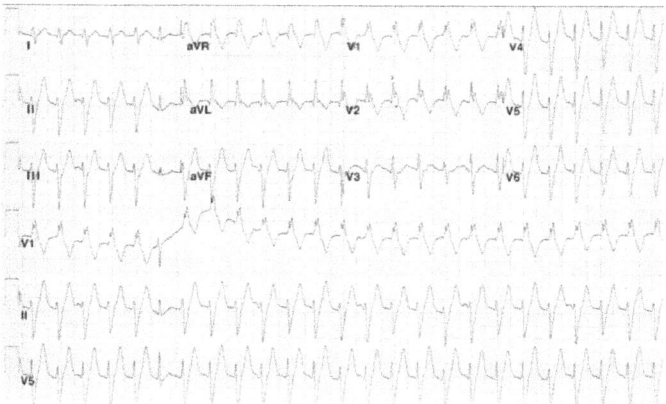

Ventricular Tachycardia – Monomorphic (VT)

Definition :-

Ventricular Tachycardia (VT) is abroad complex tachycardia originating in the ventricles. There are several different varieties of VT – the most common being Monomorphic VT.

Monomorphic ventricular tachycardia Clinical Significance

- Ventricular tachycardia may impair cardiac output with consequent hypotension, collapse, and acute cardiac failure. This is due to extreme heart rates and lack of coordinated atrial contraction (loss of "atrial kick").

- The presence of pre-exciting poor ventricular function is strongly associated with cardiovascular compromise.

- Decreased cardiac output may result in decreased myocardial perfusion with degeneration to VF.

- Prompt recognition and initiation of treatment (e.g. electrical cardioversion) is required in all cases of VT.

Ventricular Tachycardia classification is based on:
Morphology
- Monomorphic
- Polymorphic VT
- Torsades De Pointes (Polymorphic with QT prolongation)
- Right Ventricular Outflow Tract
- Tachycardia
- Fascicular Tachycardia
- Bidirectional VT
- Ventricular Flutter
- Ventricular Fibrillation

Causes of Monomorphic VT
- Ischaemic Heart Disease
- Dilated cardiomyopathy
- Hypertrophic cardiomyopathy
- Chaga's Disease

Duration
- Sustained = Duration >30 seconds or requiring intervention due to haemodynamic compromise.
- Non-sustained = Three or more consecutive ventricular complexes terminating spotaneously in <30 seconds.

Clinical Presentation
- Haemodynamically stable.
- Haemodynamically unstable – e.g. hypotension, chest pain, cardiac failure, decreased conscious level

Electrocardiographic Features of Ventricular Tachycardia

Ventricular tachycardia can be difficult to differentiate from other causes of broad complex tachycardia. The following characteristics aid in the identification of VT.

Features common to any broad complex tachycardia:
- Rapid heart rate (>100bpm).
- Broad QRS complexes (>120ms)

Features of suggestive of VT
- Very broad complexes(>160ms).
- Absence of typical RBBB or LBBB morphology.
- Extreme axis deviation ("northwest axis") – QRS is positive in aVR and negative in I + aVF.
- AV dissociation (P and QRS complexes at different rates).
- Capture beats – occur when the sinoatrial node transiently 'captures' the ventricles, in the midst of AV dissociation, to produce a QRS complexof normal duration.

- Fusion beats – occur when a sinus and ventricular beat coincide to produce a hybrid complex of intermediate morphology.

- Positive or negative concordance throughtout the chest leads, i.e. leads V1-6 show entirely positive (R) or entirely negative (QS) complexes, with no RS complexes seen.

- Brugada's sign – The distance from the onset of the QRS complex to the nadir of the S-wave is >100ms.

- Josephson's sign – Notching near the nadir of the S-wave.

- RSR' complexes with a taller "left rabbit ear". This is the most specific finding in favour of VT. This is in contrast to RBBB, where the right rabbit ear is taller.

Monomorphic VT

- Regular rhythm.

- Originates from a single focus within the ventricles.

- Produces uniform QRS complexes within each lead – each QRS is identical (except for fusion/capture beats).

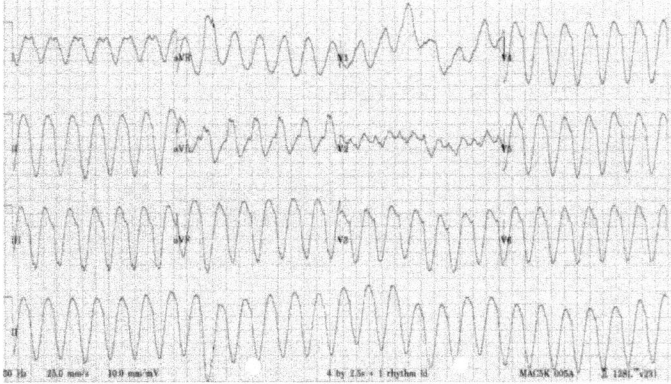

Right Ventricular Outflow Tract (RVOT) Tachycardia

Introduction

Right ventricular outflow tract (RVOT) tachycardia is a form of monomorphic VT originating from the outflow tract of the right ventricle occasionally from the tricuspid annulus. It is usually seen in patients without underlying structural heart disease, although may also occur in the context of arrhythmogenic right ventricular dysplasia (ARVD).

Diagnostic features

- Heart rate >100bpm.
- QRS duration > 120ms.
- LBBB Morphology.
- Rightward /inferior axis (around +90degree).
- Atrioventricular dissociation.

Other general features of VT, such as fusion and capture beats may also be present.

Causes

RVOT tachycardia is associated with two conditions. RVOT may be precipitated in both patient groups by catecholamine excess, stress, and physical activity:

Idiopathic VT:-

- Occurs in structurally normal hearts.
- Accounts for 10% of all VT.
- 70% of idiopathic VT will have a RVOT morphology.
- Underlying mechanism of c-AMP mediated triggered activity.
- May respond to adenosine.

Arrhythmogenic Right Ventricular Dysplasia

- An inherited myocardial disease associated with paraoxysmal ventricular arrhythmias and sudden cardiac death.
- Characterized pathologically by fibro-fatty replacement of the right ventricular myocardium.

Rhythms

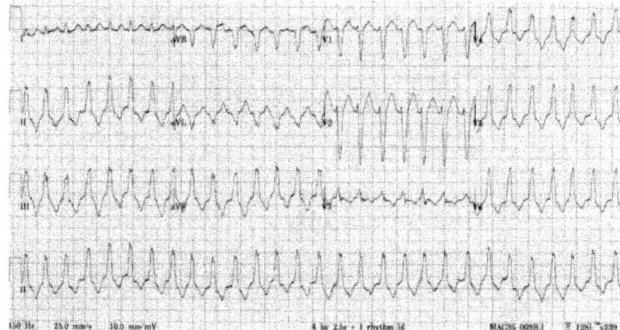

VT versus SVT

There are three main diagnostic possibilities:
1) Ventricular tachycardia (VT)
2) Supraventricular tachycardia (SVT) with aberrant conduction due to bundle branch block
3) SVT with aberrant conduction due to the Wolf-Parkinson-White syndrome

The most important distinction is whether the rhythm is ventricular (VT) or supraventricular (SVT with aberrancy), as this will significantly influence how you manage the patient. SVTs usually respond well to AV-nodal blocking drugs, whereas patients with VT may suffer precipitous haemodynamic deterioration if erroneously administered an AV-nodal blocking agent.

Unfortunately, the electrocardiographic differentiation of VT from SVT with aberrancy is not always possible.

ECG features increasing the likelihood of VT

Eletrocardiographic features that increase the likelihood of VT:

- Absence of typical RBBB or LBBB morphology
- Extreme axis deviation ("northwest axis") – QRS is positive in aVR and negative in I +aVF.
- Very broad complexes (>160ms)

- AV dissociation (P and QRS complexes at different rates)

- Capture beats – Occur when the sinoatrial node transiently 'Captures' the ventricles, in the midest of AV dissociation, to produce a QRS complex of normal duration.

- Fusion beats – occur when a sinus and ventricular beat coincides to produce a hybrid complex.

- Positive or negative concordance throughout the precordial (chest) leads, i.e. leads V1-6 show entirely positive (R) or entirely negative (QS) complexes seen.

- Brugada sign – The distance from the onset of the QRS complex to the nadir, of the S-wave is >100ms

- Josephson sign – Notching near the nadir of the S-wave

- RSR' complexes with a taller left rabbit ear. This is the most specific finding in favour of VT. NOTE: This is contrast to RBBB, where the right rabbit ear is taller.

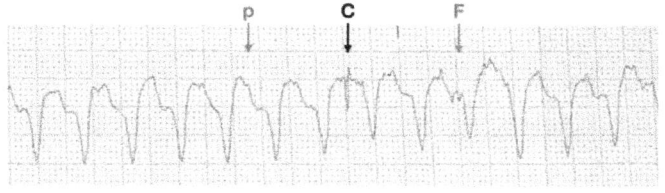

p   p wave in AV dissociation   C **Capture beat**   F Fusion beat

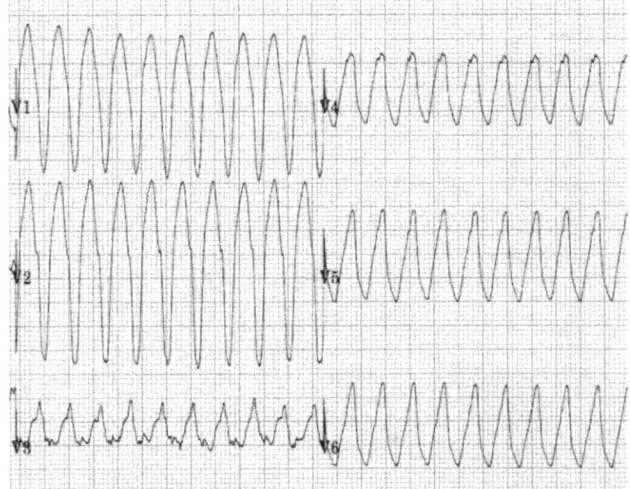

Positive concordance throughout the precordial leads:

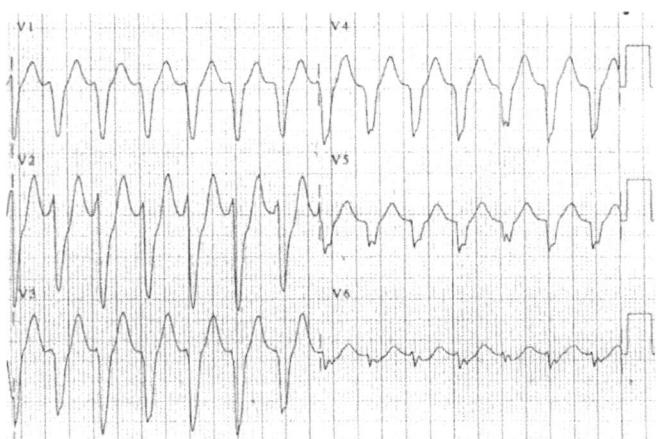

Negative concordance throughout the precordial leads:
Negative concordance in VT: Leads V1-6 show entirely negative (QS) complexes, with no RS complexes seen.

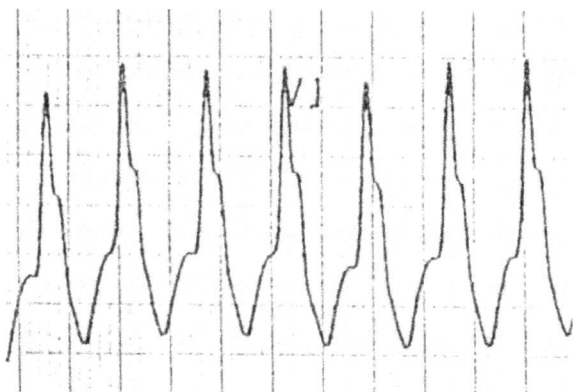

RSR' complexes with a taller left rabbit ear:

This is the most specific finding in favour of VT

This is in contrast to RBBB, where the right rabbit ear is taller.

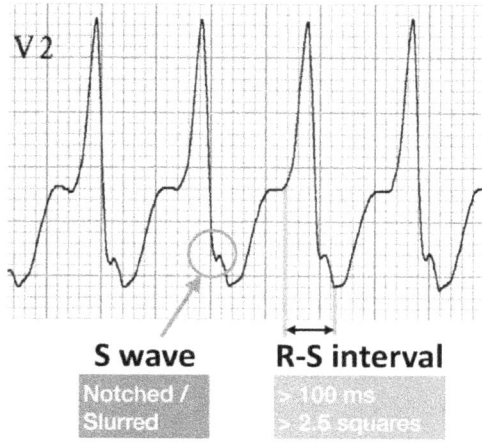

Lead V2 demonstrating both Josephson sign (blue) and Brugada sign (green).

www.ingramcontent.com/pod-product-compliance
Lightning Source LLC
LaVergne TN
LVHW061540070526
838199LV00077B/6851